FIRST-ORDER PRINCIPLES FOR COLLEGE TEACHERS

First-Order Principles for College Teachers
Ten Basic Ways to Improve the Teaching Process

ISBN 1-882982-12-6

Composition by Deerfoot Studios
Cover design by Deerfoot Studios

Anker Publishing Company, Inc.
176 Ballville Road
P.O. Box 249
Bolton, MA 01740-0249

FIRST-ORDER PRINCIPLES FOR COLLEGE TEACHERS

Ten Basic Ways to Improve the Teaching Process

Robert Boice
State University of New York - Stony Brook

ANKER PUBLISHING COMPANY, INC.
Bolton, MA

Dedicated to Elisabeth Knapp, Grand Rapids Junior College:

My most caring, effective, and inspiring teacher

ABOUT THE AUTHOR

Bob Boice is professor of psychology at the State University of New York at Stony Brook. He has published over 200 articles in scholarly journals (e.g., *Journal of Higher Education, Psychological Bulletin, Teaching of Psychology,* and *Behaviour Research & Therapy*) and numerous books (e.g., *The New Professor,* Jossey-Bass; *Developing a Diverse Faculty* [with Joanne Gainen], Jossey-Bass; *How Writers Journey to Comfort and Fluency,* Praeger; and *Procrastination and Blocking,* Praeger). He has also headed faculty development programs for almost 30 years: at SUNY Stony Brook; University of Missouri, Columbia; SUNY Albany; and California State University, Long Beach. He is the proud recipient of teaching honors…and the much prouder mentor of many graduate students and junior faculty who have won teaching awards. His passions include restoring antique cars and radios, growing day lilies, reading travel adventures, writing, dogs, and—of course—teaching.

Contents

Introduction:
Why Fundamentals?

The answer is fundamental. First-order principles of college teaching can be the easiest route to working happily and successfully in the classroom. They are an effective way to begin finding comfort and competence as a teacher. They set the stage for mastering more complex teaching skills. They ensure good beginnings (or rebeginnings). First things first.

WHAT ARE FIRST-ORDER PRINCIPLES?

First-order principles (FOPs) are uncomplicated and essential but traditionally overlooked; most of us learn them by trial and error, if at all. Why do I think they are important? In a decade of analysis of college teachers who make successful versus difficult starts, I found FOPs more telling than anything else teachers did.

Even though we may dislike labeling teaching as "work," its mastery depends on learning basic skills of working that usually remain tacit and untaught. The best, most creative, and satisfied teachers, in my experience, learn how to work at their craft. Ordinarily, we don't teach ourselves or our students much about how to work at academic tasks. And so it is, I contend, that too few of us in or near the professoriate find enough success in teaching.

FOPs are as elementary as the kinds of pacing and patience that limit fatigue and enhance student involvement. (As in calming, slowing, listening, and reflecting.) FOPs are as easily seen, once we know what to look for, as the positive/prosocial motivators that minimize classroom incivilities. FOPs are neither glamorous nor quick; they take time and practice, but they bring surprising success and joy to teaching. And even if you suppose you have too little time or need to practice FOPs, know this: without them you will probably waste far more time on inefficiencies such as preparing too much material for classes, working too hard and too unimaginatively, struggling to effect approval and learning in remote students, searching for ways to get out of teaching.

Basic Assumptions

This is my premise: When college teachers do not learn FOPs, they risk inefficiency and frustration; with FOPs, they find quicker and easier success. It's a fact. Examples: FOPs engender more reflective and creative lecture preparation done early, in small bits. They elicit more student comprehension from classes broken into brief, succinct segments with clear and memorable messages. And FOPs are economical: they produce more from less. They even prime us to master more complex skills such as teaching critical thinking and problem solving.

Said another way, FOPs are more about learning to work efficaciously than about content issues; they are more about the process of teaching than the product. Content tends to be more specific to disciplines and types of courses, even to the idiosyncratic styles of teachers. Here we look for simple generalities.

One more thing: FOPs are redundant. Each new FOP overlaps with and repeats parts of other FOPs. They, like this little book, require patience and trust. Patience—to rehear and reconsider principles that initially sound too counterintuitive or self-evident for careful listening. Trust—to take the plunge and try some ideas and strategies that will seem foreign to many teachers. While you may profit from a brisk perusal of the pages ahead, real benefit will await more patient and tolerant immersion. Go slowly, surely. At least that is what the great majority of my program participants have indicated.

Why FOPs are Relatively New to Advice Books for College Teachers

The first reason why FOPs are not well-known is that tradition supposes that while good teaching can be learned, it cannot be taught, at least not beyond a few tips about how to handle predictable necessities such as student cheating. Thus, college teaching has been treated as something to be grasped by trial and error if at all, and as something to be inspired, almost evangelically.

The result is predictable: tradition holds that there are no basic rules about teaching well, that everyone and every course occasions so different a teaching style that few, if any, generalities can be drawn. So it is that tradition offers mostly superficial, anecdotal sorts of advice. In the main, it treats only the symptoms of bad teaching, after the fact, with guesses about better problem solving strategies, such as admonitions to maintain eye contact with students, but without first helping teachers find the comfort and confidence to do so; or, criticisms of usual tendencies to lecture without first showing teachers how to conduct something that they may never have seen—effective discussions.

The second reason why FOPs have been overlooked is that we didn't have many facts about them until recently. In all the thousands of articles about college teaching, only a few have shown documented ways of improving it in enduring, substantial ways. Amazing but true. No wonder the professoriate hasn't taken advice books or programs seriously.

New Findings About Improving Teaching

Consider one example of these new findings. The first systematic studies of how new graduate students and faculty learn to teach are illuminating, but they remain obscure (I know because I have published some of them). Briefly, these observations suggest:

- "Quick starters" (newcomers who rate highly on a variety of dimensions during their first few years on campus) are distinctively consistent and economical in the practice of their basics (FOPs).

- Quick starters provide a compellingly useful picture of efficient ways to learn to teach.

- The most telling FOPs are simple skills that can also help peers who make less favorable beginnings. Perhaps good teachers are born, but they can also be made.

These studies also indicate that FOPs are essential to a broad variety of teachers and settings. FOPs work for almost everyone, even skeptics and cynics. And, most germane to this little book, research shows that the essential skills and attitudes of FOPs can be compressed into a short list of 10 memorable rules. Broader inquiries of this sort indicate that sharing the tacit knowledge of success helps in problem solving and other academic spheres where too many people have to learn the hard way, usually painfully and incompletely (Boice, 1993b).

The ten FOPs, as you might have gathered, are the essence of this book.

Why FOPs Prove Tolerable

Let me recount the ways:

- FOPs bring the fastest, easiest, success in classroom performances.

- The same elementary skills generalize to other demanding tasks such as scholarly writing (more about this later).

- FOPs provide a sound basis for making better use of more traditional kinds of advice about teaching improvement.

- FOPs are effective and economical. They take little time and soon save more than they take; their practice requires only a few minutes a day and produces quick, pleasant results. FOPs can benefit many teachers who dare even a brief look—some readers, in my experience, need time to contemplate the scheme before they will try it; some need to experience teaching to see how and where the FOPs could work.

Why FOPs May Seem Initially Objectionable

Tradition dissociates efficiencies from teaching. Seemingly, brilliant teaching is completely idiosyncratic, without many rules or constraints, without concern for businesslike ways of working. It is mysterious and manageable by only those with the gift. But if we look at conclusions about better-regarded, better-studied parts of academic work, we might wonder why they couldn't apply to teaching:

> *Physics is experience, arranged in economical order.*
> Ernst Mach

So, I would argue, is good teaching.

The Plan for this Book: First Things First

Overall I have arranged the book based on what difficulties new teachers typically encounter first and which turning points are earliest and most perilsome. Throughout, I emphasize the most basic and effective FOPs. First things first.

This is the plan put simple:

We start with *classroom comfort and control*. Why? No other aspects of teaching are so fundamental, so important to enduring success. Chapter 1 is about understanding and managing classroom incivility (teachers' own and their students') by way of simple strategies of immediacy. That means putting ourselves and our students at ease by way of mutual involvement and positive communication. Chapter 2 deals with patience, pacing, and related things that also help teachers feel comfortable and in control.

Then we move to slightly more complex versions of what we have just considered, to practice *timing and rhythms of working and thinking.* Chapter 3 shows the advantages of beginning work before feeling fully ready or inspired (because the most effective, reliable motivation comes in the wake of working, not in advance of it). Chapter 4 is about the benefits of segmenting work (even classroom presentations) into briefer, better organized sections. Chapter 5 prompts ways of stopping when enough has been done for the moment or day. Timely stopping is harder and more important than starting.

Next, and inevitably (as it turns out), we cover the FOPs that are crucial once you are regularly involved in the 10 steps of the program. Two of these deal with moderating worrisome, negative thinking and overreactions as teachers (Chapters 6 and 7). Another is about letting go of some control and allowing others do some of the work (Chapter 8). Oddly enough, letting go of control to acquire even more of it is key to more productive, creative, satisfying work. (You might need to reread the last sentence to catch its Zen-like meaning.)

Finally, this book helps prepare you for the long haul as a teacher. First it coaches you to work on tolerance for new ideas and eagerness for alternative ways of working. Then it helps you to build resilience—mainly by limiting wasted effort. And lastly, it illustrates ways to base teaching improvement on more reading and research.

How to Use this Book

This book, *First-Order Principles,* is *not* designed to be read quickly, especially not in a single sitting. Instead, it aims to impart usually untaught and unwritten concepts gradually and somewhat repetitiously; many of the ideas are so counterintuitive that they take time to sink in. In my experience, the best use of this book comes in brief, regular exposures—while its rules and strategies are being tried. It is, ironically, a book about patience for often impatient readers.

Do FOPs Work?

I have, in typically repetitious fashion, already given some of this answer. FOPs provide the only documented changes of things that matter and endure in college teaching, according to research that measures dimensions such as classroom comfort, clarity/comprehension, student approval, and student learning as evidenced in notetaking. FOPs produce impressive outcomes in the subjective accounts of participants in my programs who speak of making teaching easier but better, even of excelling without having their teaching commitment interfere with research, writing, and other important activities. (Some of these data are presented in Chapter 11.)

But what might interfere with practicing the 10 FOPs? Usual prejudices condemn efficiency as dull, confining, pressuring, and demeaning. Those assumptions do not apply here, at least not rationally.

Ten FOPs for College Teaching

The following are the ten first-order principles to be explained and practiced in the chapters ahead. There are more FOPs, but these ten have proved most effective. Despite their simplicity, they often present a problem: initially, at least, they may seem cryptic and contrary.

1. Moderate CI (classroom incivilities) with Prosocial Immediacies

2. Wait

3. Begin Before Feeling Ready

4. Work and Teach in Brief, Regular Sessions

5. Stop

6. Moderate Overattachment to Content and Overreaction to Criticism

7. Moderate Negative Thinking and Strong Emotions

8. Let Others Do Some of the Work

9. Welcome Learning and Change

10. Build Resilience by Limiting Wasted Efforts

The way to make sense of these peculiar rules is to keep reading. I want, much like an effective teacher starting a class with some intriguing propositions, to have elicited enough of your curiosity and trust to keep you going. Remember: Patience, patience, patience.

PART I

The Ten First-Order Principles

1

Moderate Classroom Incivilities with Prosocial Immediacies (Rule 1)

I begin and end my account of the 10 First-Order Principles in a distinctive fashion, one intended to catch your attention (much as I do with each class meeting I teach). As part of making my case overall, I include brief accounts of scholarship and research on college teaching in Chapters 1 and 11. This is why: In each instance I sample the kinds of observations and data that buttress my advice about teaching improvement. In each case, I show why research-based information about teaching is desirable.

This first chapter, then, is an unusually thorough account, one that includes scholarly citations and research outcomes related to a most pivotal problem for new teachers: matters of classroom incivilities. Still, consistent with the spirit of this book, I keep it shorter than I would one of my journal articles. Later in the book, in Chapter 11, I end the rules by depicting how my research programs actually produce proof of teaching improvements for teachers who practice the 10 FOPs. This sort of empirical basis is new to books of advice on teaching, and it is important because it means the FOPs work; they are not based merely on conjecture or traditional beliefs.

By spacing the empirical data, I hope to strike a balance between substance and accessibility. And I hope to find a happy medium between the preferences of some readers for research/scholarly backing and of some for more action-oriented writing—much as effective teachers commonly offer changes of pace, from details to generalities. This first chapter is worth reading because its findings set the rationale for most of what follows. That is, the same FOPs that reduce incivilities also prove essential to other aspects of teaching.

Why begin this way? In my experience, the methods and facts I overview in the rest of the chapter stay with readers more than anything else in the book. Not only do teachers recall the facts behind this first FOP and notice their application to the other FOPs; they also carry out similar research projects in their own classes, as a way of verifying what I say, even of helping to specify what they themselves could do better in practicing FOPs. So even though you might feel impatient about getting to the rest of the rules, please slow down (much as you might like your students to do when they begin to grow restless during your presentations of basics).

WHY BEGIN WITH THIS FOP?

Classroom incivilities (CI) might seem a remote problem for college teachers. We know them best from news accounts about intimidation and violence directed at high school teachers. Still, in my own studies of new faculty coping as teachers, CI frequently dominated classes and often made or broke novice teachers. Indeed, CI proved to be powerful predictors of how semesters (even teaching careers) would proceed; instances of CI were the first and most important turning points, for good or for bad, that I observed in college teaching careers.

I discovered more information about CI in the literature than I had imagined available, most of it, though, from different, more indirect vantages than I had hoped. The four extant views provide a useful background for understanding CI.

CI as Taboo, as Embarrassing

Social psychologists have documented the reason why we do not persistently question people's failings or seriously examine their excuses, and why we resist admitting when we struggle with acts that presumably reveal our intelligence, including teaching. Doing so can be an embarrassment to ourselves and a social impropriety towards others (Snyder & Higgins, 1988). Nonetheless, some of our counterparts in other teaching professions do better than we at facing up to the taboo. Psychotherapists, for instance, acknowledge why they dislike admitting annoyance with difficult patients. Such a disclosure might be interpreted by colleagues as a sign of poor therapeutic skills (Fremont & Anderson, 1988).

My point in illuminating such a dark corner of professional activity is to show why we typically neglect or distance ourselves from CI. It helps explain why what we know about CI is so amiably remote: It embarrasses.

CI as More Studied/ Publicized Among
Teachers with Less Status and Privacy

In the lower grades, public accounts of student disruptiveness proliferate. News reports routinely depict urban schools, even some rural settings, in terms of insolent, indifferent students (Coles, 1993). Elementary schools now require programs of violence prevention (Goleman, 1993); students at surprisingly young ages find school a nightmarish experience of sexual and other aggressive taunts (Baringer, 1993). By early adolescence, students commonly talk about the pain of enduring mean, boring teachers—and they act in classes accordingly (Manegold, 1993). Soon after, they often demand the good grades requisite for college but without interest in learning the basics (Lee, 1993). This atmosphere, not surprisingly, demoralizes and exhausts teachers (Toby, 1993). It also sends us increasingly difficult students.

But when we look past the dramatic, we can learn practical things about the nature and prevention of CI. Disorder—both inside and outside the classroom—may engender a loss of community spirit and with it a lessening of the informal social controls that maintain interest and order. Teachers accustomed to working amid disorder suppose that little can be done to change it, and so they do less to discourage the rudeness, violence, and demoralization that follow (Toby, 1993). In settings where teachers establish truces with classes by demanding little and getting it, a few intimidating students can discourage open displays of interest in other class members. Even there, solutions for CI are possible. Briefly angry but caring confrontations with students can enable the teacher and most of the students to break the hold of fear and foreignness on both sides (Coles, 1993).

And when classes discuss what provokes anger, students share ways of resolving conflicts more peaceably (Goleman, 1993).

CI as More Readily Acknowledged Amongst Other Practitioners

We might profit, again, in looking at the experiences and reactions of other practitioners who must deal with difficult patients and clients. Physicians place most of the responsibility for misbehavior on patients; there is little onus for doctors whose patients resist and refuse to comply. Still, physicians (far more than professors) are coached in ways of reducing the stress and burnout that come with manipulative, controlling, uncooperative patients. These are common admonitions: a) understand the causes of resistance (e.g., fear and misinformation) and respond impersonally; b) balance caring with objectivity; c) have confidence you are doing the right thing; and d) find more peer support and hobbies (Smith & Stendler, 1983).

Psychotherapists model another bold move not typically considered by teachers facing resistance. They publicly acknowledge which of their patients' behaviors annoy them most (e.g., impositions such as late night, non-emergency calls) and which should be tolerated (e.g., "dynamic" struggles that patients display in working through difficult problems—Fremont & Anderson, 1988). More important, they constantly and firmly remind patients of what behaviors help or hinder therapy (Tryon, 1986).

Because of this openness and inquisitiveness, I think, therapists are far more likely than teachers to suppose that their successes rely on practicing the right skills, not on inheriting the right genes. Hill and Corbett (1993) show why the skills-approach has found widespread acceptance with therapists. Early research by Carl Rogers established the value of skills like a focused voice that has an irregular pace, moderate to high energy levels, and variable accents. Robert Carkhuff added more credibility to this skills assumption by demonstrating that early training of therapists is best aimed at teaching basic ways of working: problem solving and decision-making skills. Process researchers, as they call themselves, even demonstrate the teachability of more advanced skills. Norman Kagan pioneered research that identified two skills essential to expertise: learning to share patients' perceptions of how therapy sessions progress; and knowing how to get past performance anxieties that inhibit already learned skills.

The upshots of this tradition may be worth our notice as teachers. Therapists boast a sharing of ideas between humanists and behaviorists because the same skills prove to be essential to either approach. Said another way—empathic, warm, skilled therapists require no theoretical orientation (instead, they put more value on skills like interpretation and nonverbal immediacy—e.g., smiling, facing, moving, and moderate distancing). Where these practices are missing, Hill and Corbett note, so is adequate awareness and anticipation of client reactions, especially of the negative kind. FOPs are crucial to things other than just classroom teaching.

CI as Higher Education Approaches It
Experts on teaching, clearly, remain decades behind therapists in empirically evaluating what affects success among college teachers in domains including CI (Weimer & Lenze, 1991). And when authorities approach the awkward topic of trouble in the classroom, they do so with monumental indirectness. They talk abstractly about the breakdown of traditional student-faculty relationships but not specifically about how it demoralizes faculty (Wilson, 1990). They blame deteriorating conditions of teaching on democratic tendencies to admit underqualified students into college, without addressing the immediate problems of ever more crowded classrooms (Henry, 1994).

This same legacy, the one that perpetuates obscurity for CI, encourages another oversight: We are unaccustomed to asking questions about whether some kinds or degrees of CI might be adaptive in our classrooms. What would happen if we looked more closely? One clue lies in representations of traditionally acceptable students. They can be seen as so eager to please authority figures, so oversensitive to negative evaluations, as to approach what therapists label a dependent personality disorder (Bornstein & Kennedy, 1994). So it is, possibly, that school impresses many independent students, including the bulk of people who find greatness, as uncongenial and irrelevant (Simonton, 1994). Another irreverent hint is that traditional teachers may err in adhering too closely to academic norms of rationality, impersonality, and formality—so much so that even positive emotions are discouraged in students (Bowen, Seltzer & Wilson, 1987). What does it matter? For one thing, emotions help learners to focus attention on important topics, to persevere, and to find inspiration. For another, emotional expression makes teachers seem more human to students. And third, consider that cultures different from our own see a value for, say, emotional trash-talking as a leveler and motivator (DeJonge, 1993).

There is a point to this alternative literature: it reminds us that in looking for ways to moderate CI, we can go too far. After all, the ultimate of psychological health and functioning—self-efficacy—depends not only on success but also on learning to reinterpret stressful events in more tolerant, optimistic ways (Bandura, 1986; Perry, Hechter, Menec, & Weinberg, 1993).

Empirically-based accounts of CI. All but a few of these are generally abstract and indirect. In an extensively documented program, Amada (1992) treats CI largely as a mental health problem; more students with schizophrenia, manic-depression, and personality disorders are coming to our campuses. Their incivilities are best treated in campus mental health centers (or, in extreme cases, with legal action). What makes Amada's approach indirect and limited? The bulk of CI needs to be dealt with in and near the classroom by teachers themselves; only extremely disruptive or disturbed students require formal treatment.

Another drawback to little-known research on CI is that it tends to prove the obvious. Wyatt (1992), for example, found students more likely to cut classes they did not like. Even so, some of these confirming studies help clarify things. Examples: Not just absences but cheating (another form of CI) relate to disliking a class, particularly when students see classes as irrelevant to their careers (Didner, 1992). And, more interesting, CI can be conceptualized, at least in survey responses, to fall into three general reciprocities between students and teachers. Both especially dislike people in the other role who come to class late. Students dislike teachers who run overtime; teachers loathe class members who pack up early. And both complain about counterparts who cut or cancel classes (Appleby, 1990).

Other, more surprising research may prove even more useful. Tracking studies suggest that most newcomers to college teaching rely on their own personal experiences as students, not on direct observations of their students, to determine when difficulties are likely to arise in classes (Lenze & Dinham, 1994). Analogously, novice teachers often make erroneous assumptions about their students' prior knowledge. With the right kinds of experience, though, teachers develop enhanced sensitivity to problems such as inattention (Fogarty, Wang, & Creek, 1983). Most *uncommon* in this genre are assumptions that teachers commit classroom incivilities.

In fact, some of us are guilty of more than occasional lapses in dealing fairly and empathically with diverse students (Williams, 1994). In samplings of core courses at large, public universities, as many as a third of faculty treat students with unmistakable rudeness and condescension. In a few cases they physically assault students who press them for answers or help (Boice, 1986; 1993a), perhaps about as often as students assault professors. In many more instances professors take advantage of teaching dynamics to sexually and otherwise compromise students.

The most thorough-going researches on CI (classroom incivility). These assume that students and teachers are partners in generating and exacerbating CI. They even report its commonness and its varieties: In a typical class of thirty, five or six students resist doing what the teacher wants (and just one troublesome student can ruin an entire class for everyone). CI typically means missing classes, cheating, refusing to participate, coming unprepared, and distracting teachers and other students. Kearney and Plax (1992) remind us that some kinds of student (and teacher) resistance can be labelled constructive (as when substantive questions are pressed), even though most teachers react to any confrontation as problematic.

What other roles do teachers play? The ways in which teachers present themselves may be the most telling factor, at least in initiating CI. In laboratory simulations, Kearney and Plax found that students decide to resist and misbehave depending largely on how they interpret two interrelated kinds of teacher behaviors. One is a matter of whether the teacher employs mostly prosocial motivators (e.g., "do you understand?" and "you can do better!") or antisocial motivators (e.g., threats and guilt induction). The second factor of teacher behavior in moderating CI is immediacy—the extent to which s/he gives off verbal and nonverbal signals of warmth, friendliness, and liking (e.g., forward leans, smiles, purposeful gestures, eye contact). With positive motivators and—particularly—immediacy, student inclinations to commit CI drop off dramatically. But without these skills, teachers are seen as cold, uncaring, and incompetent by their students—as deserving targets of incivilities. So, according to Kearney and Plax, power in classrooms is relational. Teachers have the power (if they have the skills) to use motivators and immediacies to moderate CI. And students have the power (far more than most teachers appreciate) to effectively undermine teachers who seem not to care about them.

Why is research such as Kearney and Plax's important? It identifies qualities of good teaching that have gone most unnoticed in traditional, conjectural books of advice for teachers. And it specifies some of the behaviors/skills underlying effective teaching.

It is worth knowing that FOPs of immediacy can be taught. Resulting improvements bring skills to a new level—near to that already exhibited by experienced, successful teachers (Plax & Kearney, 1992) . This research on communication in teaching may be the first significant breakthrough in understanding the origins, preventives, and correctives for CI. Given that leap forward, it was easier for me to know where to begin my own studies of FOPs.

What Proves More Useful than Usual Perspectives

Consider (much as though I were pausing to review material I had just covered in a class) what we have seen in the four perspectives on CI: It seems to be increasingly problematic, at least in K-12 classes. It is usually left undiscussed, particularly in higher education. It involves common complaints such as teachers running overtime and students trying to leave early. Its costs include discomfort, danger, and derailed learning. And, while tradition holds students mostly responsible for CI, emerging research suggests that teachers' underuse of positive motivators and immediacies may be more telling. Teachers themselves can be uncivil.

A DIRECT STUDY OF CLASSROOM INCIVILITY

I began by observing inductively and theoretically, much as I once did as an ethologist learning the social dynamics of kangaroo rats and grasshopper mice. I had little idea what to expect, and I took notes on almost everything until normative behavior patterns and individual differences grew familiar. Here, though, the classes I tracked offered an advantage over the communities of desert creatures I once haunted: Students and faculty proved to be eager reporters and interpreters of CI. After two years of patient observation and discussion, I had derived a working taxonomy of CI, and I felt prepared to undertake the more formal study I overview here (a near surfeit of details can be found in Boice, 1996).

I sat near the rear of classes so that I could come and go without disturbing them. I located myself so that I could see most students while closely observing four of them at note-taking. As I made my own notes and periodic ratings, I identified students to interview after class. Weekly interviews with faculty usually took place in their offices or by phone (because immediately after classes they were typically occupied with students asking questions). In their regular meetings with me, teachers answered questions and made ratings.

General Patterns

Common perceptions of CI. Much of what I noted as instances of CI confirms the existence of the kinds suggested in the literature: e.g., both students and teachers were annoyed by late arrivals, late stopping, and each others' cutting or canceling. But these complaints were only part of the picture and evidently not the most crucial. The picture grows clearer as I move from general norms to patterns of individual differences and of their correlates.

Teachers and students agreed in ranking only these three kinds of CI as strongly disturbing:

1. Students conversing so loudly that lecturers and student discussants could not be heard throughout a third or more of class meetings

2. Students confronting teachers with sarcastic comments or disapproving groans. A typical example, one that came after teachers finished giving assignments, was the student remark "You're kidding!"...accompanied by sneers and the noises of notebooks slamming shut

3. The presence of one or perhaps two "classroom terrorists" whose unpredictable and highly emotional outbursts (such as insulting complaints or intimidating disagreements) made the entire class tense

After these three common perceptions of CI, students and teachers diverged on the rank ordering and content of other bothersome kinds.

For students, who perceived half-again as many incidents of CI as did their teachers, the following categories ranked as next most common:

4. Teachers seen as distant, cold, and uncaring; i.e., lacking in immediacy

5. Teachers who surprised them with test items and grades that they had not prepared for or anticipated

6. Teachers who came more than five minutes late to class and/or who canceled classes without advance warning

7. Students who taunted/belittled fellow class members

Teachers, in contrast, produced these fourth through seventh rankings of CI in their classes:

4. Students who seemed reluctant to participate by answering or asking questions, or reluctant to display interest

5. Students who came to class unprepared

6. Students who imposed by demanding make-up exams or extended deadlines for projects

7. Students who arrived late and left early, and disruptively

A preliminary glance at these second-level (but still intrusive) experiences of CI reveals interesting differences and similarities between students and faculty. For example, while students seemed far less likely than faculty to notice when other students were not participating in class, both sides particularly disliked classroom terrorists for the pall they cast over whole semesters.

My own classroom observations produced similarities and differences compared to the rank-orderings just seen:

1. Teachers alienating themselves from students via negative comments and non-immediate nonverbals

2. Teachers distancing themselves from students via fast-paced, non-involving lectures

3. Students conversing so loudly that lecturers and discussants could not be clearly heard

4. Students coming late and leaving early, without apparent attempts to be unobtrusive

5. Students making sarcastic remarks/gestures

6. Teachers eliciting student mistrust via surprises on tests and grading

7. Teachers and students being intimidated, distracted, and demoralized by a classroom terrorist

Why were my own conclusions different from those of the teachers and students whose classes I analyzed? (Even though students and I were closely similar in attributing the highest levels of CI to classes of teachers whom I had preselected as deficient in prior semesters.) It was a matter of timing. If I had included my earliest, pilot observations, my rank-orderings would more closely have resembled those of teachers and students (who at this stage were also inexperienced observers of CI). What became clear with systematic practice at noticing CI is the importance of its patterning over a semester. CI usually gets set in its course on the first few days of classes. Not until teachers' negativities confirm students' skepticism and exacerbate the playful or exploratory CI of settling in and of testing how teachers will respond, do incivilities become salient and problematic.

Which source of information about CI is most important? All three perspectives on CI seem vital. Not until I presented all three vantages in a follow-up semester, where teachers were looking again at CI as they taught a new round of classes, was there evidence of cognizance that translated into reliably changed practices in classrooms. I will mention more about what happens in such interventions, but here I turn to something that faculty apparently needed to appreciate beforehand: understanding what CI is, its generality among other teachers, what prices it exacts, and how students experience it. One avenue to that understanding came in realizing how students and teachers actually perceive CI. In what comes next I present only a brief sampling.

Representative Comments about CI from Students
These excerpts typify what I entered in my general notes after classes:

About how teachers seem to alienate and distance themselves from students on the first days of class: a) "He seemed very smart, very business-like. I was impressed that he talked so far over our heads. But I got the feeling that he didn't really like students, not ones like me...that was pretty much when I gave up on him and decided to lag it." b) "Who is he kidding? He doesn't want to teach us. He starts off by telling us that he won't be talking to us outside class; only his TAs will. He tells us that his lectures won't count on tests. In other words, don't bother me; don't bother to come to class. It pisses me off to think I'm paying for this....If he doesn't care, why should I?" c) "We just wasted time today. OK, so it's nice that we had a short class, but I wanted to know what it's going to be about, what the requirements are. Not a good start!" d) "It's not good when the class begins so confused. I don't think she is going to be able to handle this class; it's going to be too much for her. She lets people insult her. That's dumb." e) "I'll tell you what turned me off. He's a snob. So he went to Harvard. So? If he's so much better than us, what's he doing wasting his time here with us?" [For more examples, see Boice, 1996.]

COMMON KINDS OF CI AS PERCEIVED BY TEACHERS
About how they are perceived by students during the first few classes: a) "[shrugs] I couldn't really tell you that much. I was nervous, and I just wanted to get through it." b) "Who knows? I mean, there are definitely some in there who don't like me, or the class, or whatever. That's probably par with such poor students." c) "Really, who cares? This isn't what matters. My chairman told me not to pay too much attention to this, just to get through it." d) "There's an easy thing I learned to make a better impression. Took awhile to figure it out. I spend time finding out who they are and why they are in class. I talk about myself and why I like the course. I show them I care, and it makes a world of difference."

Interim Summary
In these general patterns, differences in student and faculty perceptions of CI were predictable. Students usually saw teachers as the main culprits, and vice-versa. But that conceptualization oversimplifies CI and makes it seem inevitable and hopeless. It casts teachers and students as natural adversaries.

Throughout the study, I noticed that some teachers (almost always those picked for having been good performers beforehand) were less affected by and less often involved in CI (even with many of the students present whom I had seen exhibiting CI with other professors). When I finally analyzed the data by subtypes and patterns (Boice, 1996), I felt reassured about prospects of depicting only some teachers in a negative way—and even then as unskilled individuals who need help in managing CI.

Specific Patterns of CI
Here, I sort out those individuals who suffered most and least from CI. I look more carefully at the roles of timing and experience in CI. I highlight some uncommon experiences (and common but generally unnoticed incidents) tied to incivility that devastate teachers. And

here, at last, I get to mention how my other observations of classroom teaching relate to CI.

New faculty versus senior faculty as teachers. Novice teachers were no more likely to have classes with markedly high levels of CI (i.e., in the top quartile of all classes so rated). Still, they (particularly those pregrouped as deficients) more often encountered it, typically for entire semesters at chronic but moderate, disheartening levels. Senior faculty evidenced a more bimodal pattern; as a rule, they either had very little CI or lots of it in their classes (overall, in accord with their predesignations as good or poor teachers). It seemed to me that senior teachers had settled into habits of liking teaching, of treating students with general enthusiasm, fondness, and immediacy—or not.

Some new faculty fell into maladaptive patterns with surprising swiftness; those who treated their undergraduates with disdain and distance approached the worst levels seen in their poorest counterparts with extensive experience. What kept disdainful, defensive newcomers from exposure to as much student CI? Students themselves suggested an answer. They could usually spot novice teachers, and they felt inclined to go easier on them (e.g., "He's new. He doesn't know better. Maybe he needs some time").

There is also a telling variation in these data that casts experience into a stronger role than I first assigned it. Senior teachers displayed more kinds of positive motivators (e.g., ways of coaching students to make better answers in class) and more depth of skill at expressing immediacies (e.g., ease at walking about the classroom and making eye contact with a variety of students). Evidently, complex skills such as composing, writing, and teaching require many years of regular, deliberate practice before true expertise is achieved (Ericsson & Charness, 1994). Only a lucky few of us ordinarily get the supports, coaching, and rewards that sustain such extensive practice (Simonton, 1994).

Role of immediacies and motivators. While the dimension of inexperience-experience mattered, it was overshadowed by the two factors predicted by Plax and Kearney (1992). What influenced CI more, evidently, were kinds of motivators used and degrees of immediacy displayed. Table 1 helps make the point by arraying my indices of motivators and immediacies against teachers partitioned by CI levels.

TABLE 1

Relationship Between Ratings of Motivation/Immediacy and CI

My Ratings of: _____

Group (and level of CI)	% of motivators used positively	level of immediacy
New Faculty (best quartile)	81%	6.2
New Faculty (worst quartile)	56%	3.7
Senior Faculty (best quartile)	93%	7.6
Senior Faculty (worst quartile)	42%	3.2

These data help buttress the other indications that teachers' own incivilities weighed heavily in CI patterns. Moreover, Table 1 reaffirms the observation that mere experience at teaching does not suffice to lessen CI. Indeed, some teachers may grow more adversarial and uncivil to their students (who respond in kind).

Role of students. The data in Table 1 leave a neighboring question unanswered. How much do students contribute to these results? The best answer may rely on analyses of how CI develops over the course of semesters.

How timing affects CI. Consider how classes in the study began. To an impressive extent, students started semesters with reserve, respect, and optimism; they were sometimes unruly (often because they were greeting friends and testing limits in playful ways). On first days of class, they showed generally moderate to low levels of CI; students waited for teachers to make the first move. Where the first few days of class were marked by conspicuously positive motivators and strong immediacies, CI dropped off to at least moderately low levels and generally stayed there; early periods in courses may have been the crucial turning point for CI. For example, teachers making good starts displayed about three instances of CI in their first class meetings, half the rate of poor starters. As semesters proceeded, counts of CI for good starters decreased while those for the worst starters increased.

Turning points. In most courses I observed, there were other crucial times in semesters. Students seemed primed to exhibit CI before and after first and second exams (especially big tests such as midterms), and near deadlines for major projects. When teachers helped prepare students for tests and projects with approximations (e.g., practice tests; preliminary deadlines for preliminary versions of projects), reactions were subdued or more optimistic. One other series of events proved pivotal: Where students got to talk with faculty outside class in friendly, egalitarian fashion, CI levels were lower. Students were candid in explaining why: "When you get to know him, he's a pretty nice guy. Not so intimidating after all....That was when I realized that he cares about students, that he wants me to do well in the course. No, now I wouldn't dream of giving him a hard time."

Uncommonly Traumatic Kinds of CI

Some of the most upsetting incidents were the least visible, the least likely to be admitted by teachers in ordinary circumstances. Usually these CIs were embarrassing and indelibly hurtful. Faculty were disconcerted by students' personal comments on formal evaluations at ends of semesters (e.g., "she dresses badly"), even when the great majority of their students' comments were positive. They often found it hard not to key-in on students who displayed especial disdain and disapproval in class ("Did you notice him? He just sits there, arms folded, glaring at me, shaking his head in disapproval."). But most devastating were incidents where students went to department chairs to complain about a teacher—and where faculty perceived that chairs assumed them guilty until proven otherwise.

In my experience, all three of these problems can be moderated by way of more humane cultural practices. Student evaluations can be screened by a neutral third party to exclude or edit personally hurtful, nonconstructive comments. Newcomers can be coached to realize that even the best teachers do not please everyone (or want to). Chairs can handle students' complaints by asking students to first discuss concerns with professors, then by approaching colleagues in ways that do not put them on the defensive (e.g., "Can you help me think what we could do to make this student happier in our classes, less likely to complain to me?").

Cheating. Another incident that demoralized teachers in two cases was student cheating; in both instances apparent culprits were defensive and angry. The tension produced in such confrontations seemed to distract these professors from their work and to exacerbate their health problems. One teacher who handled a similar problem in a way that apparently limited incivility bears mentioning: he put some of the responsibility on his students to solve the dilemma (his report to me of a private conversation: "Look, I need your help with this uncomfortable situation. The two of you turned in papers that seem very much alike. How can we figure out what happened and what to do?").

How CI (Classroom Incivility) Relates to Other Behaviors of Teachers and Students

Teaching ratings. Student ratings of teaching prowess over semesters were negatively related to levels of CI. Indeed, teachers with the lowest CI counts were rated significantly higher than peers with the highest CI levels in class on rated dimensions including these: The worth of the teaching, the suitability of the teacher's pacing to note-taking and understanding, the teacher's clarity/organization, and students' own class involvement.

Student attentiveness. Not surprisingly, background noise levels were highest in classes with high CI course ratings. In the worst examples, teachers were upstaged by a constant buzz of conversations, paper shufflings, openings of food and drink containers, fidgets, and coughs. Student attentiveness followed much the same pattern. While a minority (usually about 10-20%) of students remained obviously involved in the courses with high CI, their peers typically did not attend to the teacher or to classroom discussions with the teacher. Instead, about a third of the remainder usually sat passively, sometimes listening, sometimes closing their eyes and drowsing, sometimes looking around the room. Another third usually read or wrote for other classes, put on make-up, or ate. The final, most salient third spent most class periods conversing, greeting late comers, even moving around the room to engage new conversations.

Note taking was not a regular activity of most of the students in these classes. Undergraduates, if they took notes at all, typically entered only a few lines at the beginning of classes (e.g., announcements, assignments) and some of the salient points or diagrams or equations put on the board. That is, notes for the day usually comprised about a half-a-page in the notebooks of fifty percent of the students. (Still, I only twice saw class meetings with nothing on which to take notes.) Better note-takers (overall about a quarter of the students I observed) usually entered two or three pages of writing and diagrams, but often with little explication beyond lists, definitions, and graphics that emphasized in class. The best note-takers typically produced three to five pages in their notebooks per class. They were unique in several ways: in noting explanations and examples; in adding their own questions and reminders about what they were processing; in politely trying to interrupt professors for explanations. Better and best note-takers were, it figures, most common in the classes with the least CI.

Situations Where CI is Tolerable, Perhaps even Helpful

Earlier I suggested that CI might serve useful functions under the right conditions. In my own observations, the reality proved somewhat at odds with what I had expected. The better-rated, more "immediate" teachers simply perceived occasional, moderate incidents differently than did other teachers. If exemplary teachers noticed these disruptions as incivilities, they did not let on in class. Instead, they usually treated them respectfully, by listening carefully, as though they had been offered up as well-intentioned comments or cues. These are typical excerpts from my notes of such interactions:

- *S in row five emits loud "uugh" and sinks in his chair. T: "Oh no [laughs gently], I've worn you down, worn you out with all this. I do that sometimes. So thanks for alerting me. What do you think? Would it help if I stop and go through it again with you?"*

- *S abruptly interrupts: challenges point T just made: "I know that's wrong..." T listens cheerfully. Says: "Well, you might be right about that. I can always stand to be corrected; I can survive that. Can you come by my office and we'll share resources?"*

- *T: "I'm seeing some big yawns and abandoned note-taking. I'm sorry. I'm losing you. Let's all stand and stretch for a minute, and then we'll backtrack a bit."*

These excerpts show how teachers maintain immediacy (and its kin, optimism) through what could have been CIs but were not generally rated so by teachers or students. And they hint at how CI, in moderation, can help improve classes. Socially skilled, positive responses by teachers to student frustration help calm classrooms. They re-engage students who had been distancing themselves from the class. And according to teachers who tolerate and use them best, such distractions can, if treated imaginatively and optimistically, provide breaks in the action, even helpful cues for redirection or changed pacing.

These examples even suggest what needs to be taught to teachers without good skills/FOPs.

A Trial Program to Ameliorate Teachers' Contributions to CI (Classroom Incivilities)

Merely observing and eliciting comments about teachers' exposure to CI is an intervention. When these participants asked me, inevitably, about how often CI happened to their colleagues, my answers relieved them. Many had imagined their own experiences as unique ("You never hear such things mentioned."). When I sometimes brought up incidents that they had not noticed, they tried harder to observe and understand CI. And when, eventually, they inquired about what colleagues did to cope with CI, they typically tried emulating the strategies I summarized. This did not produce generally impressive outcomes during the same semesters; entrenched patterns of CI in such large classes are not easily turned around.

Most teachers experiencing high CI wanted to bring it under control almost immediately, and when initial attempts went badly, they resumed old styles. Still, all of these teachers expressed an interest in trying new strategies in future semesters.

The Formal Intervention Phase

I again observed, noted, and interviewed weekly. But this time I actively coached faculty with repeated reminders, before and after classes, about the general patterns of actions/attitudes that distinguished low-CI teachers. And, to make this difficult transition more realistic, I concentrated my measurements and feedback on what I assumed was the most crucial and practical category: immediacy.

- Arriving at classes early, for informal chats with students coming in the door and after they had taken seats around the room

- Deliberate practice at presenting parts of classes with active focus/moderate pacing, forward leans and open body postures, smiling and direct eye contact, walking about while lecturing/listening

- Salient reminders in written class notes of times to pause, slow, and check student note-taking for involvement/comprehension

- Taking care, in meetings with students after class and in office hours, to listen patiently and reflectively while avoiding signs of impatience (e.g., reading materials on one's desk while students talked)

Six of the ten teachers I invited as participants stayed throughout the intervention program (the other four concluded that immediacy was a dishonest expression of their personalities).

Results
All six participants showed reliably observable gains of about 30-50% in my measures of observed immediacy, with no apparent differences between four novices and two seniors who had fared badly in the prior semester. And all six evidenced far lower levels of CI than before (three in nearly identical courses; three in less demanding survey courses). So my data about the modifiability of CI in teachers and their classes are only suggestive but promising.

CONCLUSIONS ABOUT THE CI STUDY
Overall, CI was more common than uncommon; it occurred in significant ways (i.e., disruptively in at least three class meetings during a semester) in over two-thirds of the courses I tracked. Of those troubled, large survey courses, about half showed chronic, disheartening patterns of CI. In the high-CI courses, both students and faculty usually reported annoyance and demoralization. But whatever the setting, faculty (even novices who had little time to habituate to CI) noticed far less of it than did their students. And faculty took less personal responsibility for CI.

Faculty Awareness of CI
The faculty with the keenest appreciation of CI's nature and liabilities were, ironically, least likely to experience it. They were the teachers of the four courses I observed where CI was virtually absent and where other indices of teaching such as enthusiasm, pacing, and organization rated highest. Why did other faculty often overlook CI? As a rule, their attitude was reminiscent of physicians' putative reaction to resistant patients: what the teacher offers is undoubtedly valuable, and when students frustrate the teacher, the loss is only theirs. Indeed, high CI professors often acted like specialized kinds of doctors, psychoanalysts who imagined that student resistance only proved the meaningful difficulty of the material under discussion. In

their defense, though, these professors typically knew no better. Few of us talk or write much about the nature of CI or its preventives; most novice teachers I have tracked through first days of classes were simply puzzled by the ruckus in their classes. A typical comment is: "These students are certainly not the kind of student I was."

The solution that occurs to most faculty in this situation seems unacceptable. Teachers imagine that students can be won over only with pandering—easy assignments/tests and entertainment in place of serious classroom material. In the usual vicious cycle that follows, faculty often find ways to confirm this misbelief. When they alternate distant, demanding styles with periodic bouts of lowered standards (e.g., "O.K., I'll drop your lowest test score"), students quiet, but only temporarily.

Costs of CI

Another finding here is that CI matters, deeply. The differences between classrooms with a lot of CI and those without it were dramatic. With persistent CI, students grew more and more uninvolved, oppositional, and combative. Their teachers found their own seemingly innocent remarks and gestures (often emitted without their conscious awareness) escalating into adversarial interactions with students. Even when the CI was largely limited to a single, disruptive individual (what faculty and students often call a classroom terrorist), teachers were surprised to discover the increased difficulty of teaching…and that the other students held teachers responsible for not squelching the terror. Among new faculty I have tracked closely, experiences of unmanaged and unsettling CI constitute a turning point that can ruin professorial careers (Boice, 1993a). Why? New faculty tend to spend most of their time preparing for teaching (even in research universities), and when they fail at teaching, they lose the self-efficacy they need to meet challenges of research/scholarship and collegiality/professional networking. Promising newcomers who became overwhelmed by CI, too often decide to abandon professorial careers (or worse yet, resign themselves to lifetimes of marginal performance and rewards for the sake of job security). The paradox in this is that observers from a distance imagine that pressures to publish are the only villains.

Faculty Role in CI

The most important point in this study is the one usually overlooked.

Clearly, teachers were the most crucial initiators of classroom incivilities. And, as a rule, their most telling provocations occurred during
the first few days of courses. Conversely, professors who most consistently displayed immediacies and positive motivators were least
involved in incidents of CI, their own or their students'. In the intervention project I report here, teachers practicing a simple regimen of
immediacies showed clear improvements in the CI levels of their
classes. These data are not yet conclusive, but they suggest the worth
of pursuing the usually taboo topic of CI more openly and caringly.

How Much CI is Desirable?

If we agree that CI merits more study, two questions remain about
how much CI is optimal and tolerable: 1)When should we choose to
turn CI into positive communications and motivations, as did the
exemplars we saw earlier, and when should we set clear limits on its
expression? 2)When students act in racist, sexist, and other
exploitive and aggressive ways, teachers must know how to stop the
disruption dead in its tracks. What helps? This second question is no
small matter.

On most of our campuses, we are already doing some of the right
things: running seminars for faculty and students about the nature
and costs of harassment; growing pressures for teachers to begin
courses with clear explanations of what behaviors are unacceptable,
sometimes even referring to teacher behaviors; setting up easier ways
to report these forms of CI; and informing ourselves about student
diversity. One other thing may help limit intolerable CI: Classrooms
with generally low levels of CI overall had no terrorists. In this study,
the members of such courses not only scored low on dimensions like
indifference and inattention, but also gave high ratings of teachers'
use of positive motivators and immediacies. Courses with high
immediacy and low CI, so far as I can tell, somehow discourage serious incidents of incivility and terrorism. One student I had seen ter-
rorize another course suggested reasons why he did not in a course
with low levels of CI: "Everyone likes her and she cares about the students; you don't get so antsy in here."

WHAT HAVE CLASSROOM INCIVILITIES TO DO WITH YOU?

In the best of all worlds, you may encounter only the most civil, tolerant students. Or perhaps you were born so attractive and entertaining
that no one will dislike you. Even if you had all this, there would still

be reason to do the things that moderate CIs. The evidence says that your students will learn better if you display immediacies and positive motivators. And reality says that you will perform more comfortably and successfully when you do encounter students who test the limits of civility.

PRACTICES FOR RULE 1 (ANTICIPATING AND MODERATING CI)

* Observing, understanding.
* Three kinds of immediacy—arriving early and other informal interactions; forward lean, pacing, etc.; use of salient reminders to pause, slow, check.
* Monitoring results.

How should you carry out these practices? There are clues in the coverage of the CI study, above. And there are more directives, all of them related, in the FOPs ahead. The main thing is to begin to establish the habit of practicing FOPs, even their rough approximations.

In the end, this is the rule for these first steps:

Rule 1: Moderate Classroom Incivilities with Prosocial Immediacies

REFERENCES

Amada, G. (1992). Coping with the disruptive college student: A practical model. *Journal of American College Health 40*, 203-215.

Appleby, D.C. (1990). Faculty and student perceptions of irritating behaviors in the college classroom. *Journal of Staff, Program, & Organization Development* Spring, 41-46.

Astin, A.W. (1984). Student involvement: A development theory for higher education. *Journal of College Student Personnel 40*, 288-305.

Associated Press (1994). Becoming American, bad habits and all. *New York Times*, February 23, B7.

Bandura, A. (1986). *Social foundations of thought and action.* Englewood Cliffs, NJ: Prentice-Hall.

Baringer, F. (1993). School hallways as gauntlets of sexual taunts. *New York Times* , June 2, B7.

Boice, R. (1986). Faculty development via field programs for middle-aged, disillusioned faculty. *Research in Higher Education 25*, 115-135.

Boice, R. (1993a). New faculty involvement for women and minorities. *Research in Higher Education 34*, 291-341.

Boice, R. (1993b). Primal origins and later correctives for midcareer disillusionment. *New Directions for Teaching and Learning 55*. San Francisco, CA: Jossey-Bass.

Boice, R. (1996). Classroom incivilities. *Research in Higher Education*, in press.

Bornstein, R.W., & Kennedy, T.D. (1994). Interpersonal dependency and academic performance. *Journal of Personality Disorders 8*, 240-248.

Bowen, D.D., Seltzer, J., & Wilson, J.A. (1987). Dealing with emotions in the classroom. *The Organizational Behavior Teaching Review 7* (20), 1-14.

BQ (1990). Suggestions for responding to disruptive classroom behavior. *The Campus Chronicle*, April 27, 3-4.

Cohen, P. (1981). Student ratings of instruction and student achievement: A meta-analysis of multisection validity studies. *Review of Educational Research 51*, 281-309.

Coles, R. (1993). When volunteers are sorely tested. *Chronicle of Higher Education 39*(35), A52.

DeJonge, P. (1993). Talking trash. *New York Times Magazine*, June 6, 30-38.

Didner, J. (1992). Survey reveals high level of academic fraud. *Stony Brook Statesman*, February 10, 3.

Ericsson, K.A., & Charness, N. (1994). Expert performance: Its structure and acquisition. *American Psychologist 49*, 725-747

Fogarty, J.L., Wang, M.C., & Creek, R. (1983). A descriptive study of experienced and novice teachers' interactive thoughts and actions. *Journal of Educational Research 77*, 22-32.

Fremont, S.K., & Anderson, W. (1988). Investigation of factors involved in therapists' annoyance with clients. *Professional Psychology: Research and Practice 19*, 330-335.

Goleman, D. (1993). Schools try to tame violent pupils one punch and taunt at a time. *New York Times*, August 19, B11.

Henry, W.A. (1994). *In defense of elitism*. New York, NY: Doubleday.

Hill, C.E., & Corbett, M.M. (1993). A perspective on the history of process and outcome research in counseling psychology. *Journal of Counseling Psychology 40*, 3-24.

Johnson, R., & Butts, D. (1983). The relationships among college science student achievement, engaged time, and personal characteristics. *Journal of Research in Science Teaching 20*, 357-366.

Kearney, P., & Plax, T.G. (1992). Student resistance to control. In V.P. Richmond, & J.C. McCroskey. (Eds.), *Power in the classroom*. Hillsdale, NJ: Erlbaum.

Lee, F.R. (1993). Disrespect rules. *New York Times Education Supplement*, 16.

Lenze, L.F., & Dinham, S.M. (April 1994). Examining pedagogical knowledge of college faculty new to teaching. Paper presented at the American Educational Research Association, New Orleans.

Manegold, C.S. (1993). To Crystal, 12, school serves no purpose. *New York Times*, April 8, A1 & B7.

Pace, R.C. (1984). *Measuring the quality of college student experiences. An account of the development and use of the college student experiences questionnaire.* Los Angeles, CA: UCLA Higher Education Research Institute.

Pascarella, E.T., & Terenzini, P.T. (1991). *How college affects students.* San Francisco, CA: Jossey-Bass.

Perry, R.P., Hechter, F.J., Menec, V.H., & Weinberg, L.E. (1993). Enhancing achievement, motivation, and performance in college students: An attributional retraining perspective. *Research in Higher Education 34,* 687-723.

Plax, T.G., & Kearney, P.K. (1992). Teacher power in the classroom. In V.P. Richmond, & J.C. McCroskey (Eds.), *Power in the classroom.* Hillsdale, NJ: Erlbaum.

Simonton, D.K. (1994). *Greatness.* New York, NY: Guilford.

Smith, R.J., & Stendler, E.M. (1983). The impact of difficult patients upon treaters. *Bulletin of the Menninger Clinic 47,* 107-116.

Snyder, C.R., & Higgins, R.L. (1988). Excuses: Their effective role in the negotiation of reality. *Psychological Bulletin 104,* 23-35.

Tinto, V. (1975). Dropout from higher education: A theoretical synthesis of recent research. *Review of Educational Research 45,* 89-125.

Toby, J. (1993). Everyday school violence: How disorder fuels it. *American Educator 17*(4), 4-9 & 44- 47.

Tryon, G.S. (1986). Abuse of therapists by patients: A national survey. *Professional Psychology: Research and Practice 17,* 357-363.

Weimer M., & Lenze, L.F. (1991). Instructional interventions: A review of the literature on efforts to improve instruction. In J.C. Smart. (Ed.), *Higher education: Handbook of theory and research.* New York, NY: Agathon.

Williams, J.A. (1994). *Classroom in conflict: Teaching controversial subjects in a diverse society.* Albany, NY: SUNY Press.

Willis, D. (1993). Academic involvement at university. *Higher Education 25,* 133-150.

Wilson, R. (1990). Quality of life said to have diminished on U.S. campuses. *Chronicle of Higher Education 36*(33), A1 & A32.

Wilson, R., Gaff, J., Dienst, R., Wood, L., & Bavry, J. (1975). *College professors and their impact on students*. New York, NY: Wiley.

Wyatt, G. (1992). Skipping class: An analysis of absenteeism among first-year students. *Teaching Students 20*, 201-207.

2

Wait
(Rule 2)

Teachers, even novices, know how to wait in the usual sense. They wait passively and hope that success at teaching will come to them as a natural part of experience, without deliberate attempts to improve. Or they may assume they already know how to teach and that they only need await ideal circumstances for their brilliance to show itself. Both kinds of teachers want mastery to come quickly and spontaneously, without much deliberate planning or reliance on help. Sometimes this magic happens, but not usually. Instead, teachers who begin with this curious combination of passivity and impatience typically fail to make good starts or to change significantly over their careers. Their teaching remains largely private (except with those transients called students) and unsatisfying; eventually this sort of waiting makes retirement its goal.

There is another problem with passive waiting: It fosters procrastination. When we wait passively for something to happen spontaneously, we tend to spend our time on easier, unnecessary, and inefficient activities that postpone real work on teaching (Boice, 1996b). So, for example, we might wait for student acceptance while ever-refining our lecture notes to eliminate all errors of fact. The more difficult, more delayable task (one we might ordinarily procrastinate) is finding which of our materials are best understood by students and why.

There is even a third problem with passive waiting. It misleads with its sense of seeming freedom (to do whatever we want, without constraints) because it eventually leaves teachers feeling doubtful about competence. When, after waiting too long, class materials are prepared hurriedly, under deadlines, they often suffer in terms of clarity or logical flow. And where teachers cannot make the leap to the next point or tie materials to the broader picture, self-consciousness and blocking occur. In the long run, passive waiting often exposes teachers to a cruel and inefficient oppression—the rushing and forcing of deadlines to prepare for classes, even to go to them. When we have waited passively, other maladaptive things happen:

- We prepare at the last minute, hurriedly and without reflection.

- Our presentations are rushed and exhausting.

- Our students strain to keep up, and they grow more and more uninvolved.

- We perpetuate the anxieties that accompany nonreflective presentations and unresponsive audiences.

- We work at teaching as though constantly rushed and busy, and so we remain unlikely to set clear goals for classes or for our own improvements as teachers.

- (And in the terms of Chapter 1) Our rushed, impatient styles are short on immediacies.

Active Waiting

What makes active waiting different from the passive kind? It means getting ready, often implicitly and preliminarily, while waiting. So at first, active waiting seems more difficult and time consuming.

Just as important, active waiting requires patience. It means waiting and reflecting and preparing ideas and other material for teaching without impulsive rushing. It means taking the time to test lecture and discussion materials to see which of them will engage students as active learners who comprehend—before settling on classroom content. And active waiting even extends to actual teaching: It includes the patience of presenting materials slowly and clearly enough to promote ready comprehension in almost all students.

Said another way, active waiting requires the patience of not trying to prepare or present everything you know. Active waiting, because it promotes early and informal starts, brings the kind of reflectiveness essential to good decision-making and economical presentation.

Active Waiting Aims for Long-Term Rewards

Active waiting requires the kind of patience that tolerates short-term discomforts (such as temptations to do something else more immediately rewarding than preparing for teaching) in order to gain longer-term rewards (e.g., students who learn more). Active waiting means subduing the part of yourself that admonishes you to put off thoughts of teaching improvements until you are completely caught up on other things. Active waiting, surprisingly, means being able to do two or more things at once (e.g., preparing for teaching during the little openings that occur even during busy days, while nonetheless making enough progress on other things). Oddest of all, active waiting also means suspending disbelief. You might, for instance, believe that efficiencies could work for other people but not for you ("I've always been kind of disorganized and happily behind schedule; I could never stand this").

Active Waiting, Then, Is a Matter of
Pausing Reflectively and Preparing Preliminarily

It means starting preparations well before formal sessions of working on teaching (e.g., by merely inducing us to think and notice during lulls in other activities). It helps teachers spend more of their preparation time on finding imagination and motivation through the playful, unrushed organization of materials.

Active Waiting is Economical

Because this patient reflection helps simplify material by way of repeated exposures and reexaminations, lectures can be presented with fewer main points and more explanations of each. And when the preparations are patient, simple, and reflective, so are the presentations. Teachers who learn to pause and notice during preparations show the same kinds of timing and listening in class.

As a result of these economies, the pace is less taxing for teacher and students. The enjoyment of teaching grows for both sides. The students learn and retain more.

Active Waiting Is Educational

Active waiting also facilitates learning for the teacher. It teaches you what kinds of active waiting work best for you; for example, calming and slowing in class while taking time to consider links between points you've made; pausing until students solve problems. It coaches you to examine what goals (if any) you are setting for student learning, while preparing reflectively and patiently. It encourages playfulness and discovery during work at teaching. And, active waiting helps moderate the perfectionism that pressures many of us to suppose that we should make no mistakes, that we must know everything, that we ought to be in constant control.

Active waiting works because it softens its opposites, perfectionism and impatience. Patience—not impatience—fosters playfulness, tentativeness, and tolerance.

Make haste slowly
Boileau

Other Benefits of Active Waiting

Active waiting has many other benefits, some of them hard to imagine until experienced. It brings serenity because it is neither tense nor pressing. It provides a growing mindfulness of having something important and worthwhile to say before saying it. It promotes a more casual but focused attitude toward preparing and presenting; teaching that once had to be written out is now more easily and enjoyably done from conceptual outlines and diagrams that often fill but a page per class. With active waiting, decisions about the final structure of the content are put off, classes are more spontaneous and more likely to involve students as active participants. And, not least, with active waiting there is more opportunity for discovery in teaching.

Discovery proves to be so much fun that it generates enthusiasm and hooks people on teaching, even on campuses where teaching is not overtly rewarded. One more advantage of active waiting is worth mentioning: Teachers who practice it get reliably higher ratings by their students (Boice, 1995a).

WHAT HAPPENS WITHOUT ACTIVE WAITING

Few of us manage patience easily. My two decades of observing college classrooms suggest that impatience is the single most common problem among teachers. We already recognize most of the scenario from first- or second-hand experience: Lecturers begin the semester by rushing into content without having established the immediacies and ground rules that minimize incivilities. They hurry through material and communicate their dislike for being interrupted in subtle and overt ways. Then they wonder why their students grow more and more distant and uninvolved, even disapproving and uncivil. And, ultimately, they find teaching exhausting and unrewarding.

Last-Minute Work

Waiting passively until the last minute to prepare lectures and then looking down to read the lecture notes is only the beginning. Pacing accelerates as less notice is taken of student reactions and comprehension. And in the rush of things, teachers often lose track. Then they find they suddenly have to figure out what to say *as* they are saying it—without the prefiguring, planning, and rehearsals that come with active waiting. In the narrowed and painful self-consciousness that follows, they lose all hope of speaking fluently, of attending to audience reactions, or even of enjoying teaching. Simply imagining all this is a start toward more active waiting. Why? It shows us the wastefulness of passive waiting.

Teaching Anxiety

The most anxious, unsuccessful speakers show remarkably similar patterns to those of teachers who wait passively. They put off preparations (in passive fashion) until, pressed for time, they formulate something hurried and formulaic. They give little reflection to moving beyond old problem presentations in preparing their talks, particularly to how their audiences will react. Then with the time for presentation growing near, their anxiety grows with astonishing vigor. The speaker's consciousness is narrowed, and he or she cannot think ahead adaptively. More likely, thoughts will turn to hopes of magic: that once underway, the material will somehow coalesce into an inspired and brilliant whole.

Even if this seeming sorcery happens occasionally, it is too unreliable to help speakers find confidence and adaptive habits of presenting. Why? Speakers with poor work habits place additional loads on themselves. They do not prepare in flexible and sensitive ways that allow redirection at midstream or interaction with audiences. They present with a tension that discomforts their audiences and exhausts themselves. And, they remain busy trying to figure out what to say as they say it—an ideal condition for anxiety and blocking. What works better? The preliminaries that come with active waiting and generate already simplified, organized ideas: Active waiting.

Why is Active Waiting Unfamiliar?

We may know part of the reason. We take the seeming efficacy of passive waiting for granted. We are not taught to notice how passivity and impatience work quietly but in vicious circles. The more we repeat them, unthinkingly, the harder it is to break away from them. Together, they impulsively, unconsciously push us into all-or-nothing stances that usually opt for short-term rewards and even more impatience. The impulsiveness of passive waiting lies unseen, as a rule, until it impels us to act without reflection or under deadlines. It convinces us we are too busy—or too proud—to work serenely at teaching with something as presumably silly as active waiting.

So, the impatience tempts us to put off preparation for teaching (and work at improving our teaching) in favor of other, seemingly more pressing acts. And it inclines us to expect immediate, almost perfect results at teaching (ironically, all the more so when we have waited passively and prepared anxiously). Its narrowness discourages us from taking a broad look at it. As a rule, we know less about our impatience than about any other part of ourselves.

Active waiting is unfamiliar, but it is far more effective than passive waiting. I'll remind you why:

- Active waiting finds time for small, informal beginnings.

- It encourages playful and reflective approximations to what will be done during serious work sessions.

- It makes the actual doing inseparable from the pleasant preparations and, so, easier and better.

Traditional advice and books about teaching rarely say much about the importance of patience and active waiting. Custom directs novices to pay more attention to content (e.g., how to organize lecture material), to style (e.g., how to dress), and to specific problem solving strategies (e.g., how to start discussions by using provocative material). In fact, newcomers would do better to begin with more efficient ways of working, starting with general modes such as the patience of active waiting.

Impatience, that secret ingredient of passive waiting, hinders teachers from accepting help (including the sort in this book). The real difficulty about finding more patience is simple and difficult at the same time: The topic of patience may make all of us even more impatient, at least in the short run. Ordinarily, we prefer not to mention it, and we overestimate the difficulty of vanquishing it. Yet, once in practice, it reinforces itself.

WHAT HAPPENS WITH ACTIVE WAITING

The kinds of patience you'll develop here as part of active waiting are not all that arduous. At first they require little more than pauses for relaxing and resetting pacing to a slower, calmer gait. Invariably, they impel you to put off closure about what you will do. But the FOP of active waiting does not get in the way of other important things or take more time in the long run. And, most surprisingly, this FOP proves enjoyable.

You might recognize a tone to all this that usually remains foreign to advice about teaching. In many ways, active waiting is like ancient notions from Yogi and Buddhist thinkers. They see active waiting even more simply, as a matter of paying attention to the moment:

> *To find our way, we will need to pay more attention to this moment. It is the only time that we have in which to live, grow, feel, and change....There is nothing passive about it. And when you decide to go [once having mindfully attended to the moment], it's a different kind of going because you stopped. The stopping actually makes the going more vivid, richer, more textured.*
>
> Jon Kabat-Zinn

The practices for this FOP require little more than brief, daily sessions of practice—so brief that they do not interfere with other important activities. What can make these practices difficult is something so elemental that we often overlook it: We must let go. Let go of what? Of the controlling feeling that impatience brings in the short run. All this can be said most simply as a rule:

Rule 2: Wait

PRACTICES FOR RULE 2

There are three of these. I recommend trying them in order without expecting them to work perfectly, at least in the short run. In actual practice, most teachers I have known rework the scheme to suit themselves. That makes sense because the point of this program is to induce you to learn reflective practices, not just my set of rules.

First, Pause to Reflect Before Writing or Talking

In other words, *wait*. Yes, actually pause for a moment. Be a little more patient. And use these brief pauses to slow down and calm down to sketch ideas, diagrams. Use them to talk to yourself and make notes, about what you could say in class. Use them to notice what you could say before saying it—to imagine talking it with your students and thinking about how they will react.

This sort of initial pause helps in several noticeable ways. I encourage you to look for the following changes:

- A growing reflectiveness that helps simplify teaching materials to their essentials. Calm, contemplative teachers are more likely to organize lectures and discussions into a few central points they hope to make for the day. For example, they replace the additional points they were tempted to make with more examples and applications of the central points.

- A slower, more deliberate style that makes teaching materials less rigid in structure and more creative. In your classroom this kind of patient flexibility generates more spontaneity of presentation and more involvement by students. Because spontaneity brings discovery, teaching becomes more exciting and enjoyable.

- A reduction in tension and fatigue. In the short run, at least, the act of noticing how well the strategies work is crucial to their success. Another thing that helps is knowing what to anticipate.

Remind yourself that practicing that habitual pausing may initially annoy you. Exercises in patience are, as we have seen, least attractive when we are in impatient moods. So to get past that usual impatience start out with moves that ensure small successes—with easy pauses, maybe no more than five minutes of reflection before formally writing out classroom materials. Start out with a brief pause at the outset of a class, perhaps for 5 to 10 seconds before beginning. Use that time to calm yourself, to establish prosocial communication by way of making eye contact and smiling. Use that pause to foster a reasonable, unrushed pace once talking.

Try using the pauses before preparing classroom materials playfully and planfully. Instead of writing or diagraming finished copy immediately, make preliminary notes, doodles, and diagrams about what you could write and say. This generally requires only a few minutes. Take a playful stance in organizing your material, one that might suggest new ways of seeing the message you hope to impart. Most important, use this time to begin to clarify your goals for a class you will be preparing more formally later on. Reflect on what, specifically, you want students to learn. A common problem of college teachers is that even when they have prepared beautifully organized notes, they lack clear learning goals. It is never too early to initiate planning and goal-setting.

Remind yourself of what expert problem solvers do. They take time to pause and to consider alternatives, to make sure they are solving the right problem or answering the right question, even to ask "why am I doing this?" They ask, "Is this, eventually, going to be some of my better, more rewarding work?"

One of the easiest ways to practice the combination of pausing and informal preparations (i.e., active waiting) is to put your first thoughts about a new or revised lecture into freewriting. Freewriting is whatever comes to mind without worrying about correctness and neatness and without listening to your internal editors. You might even begin with a bit of free talking, saying aloud the ideas and plans you have before writing them down. Either method produces a dramatic increase in your ability to listen to yourself and to discover what you have to say. Both of these methods of "letting go" are particularly useful in uncovering ideas that occur to you after those that you might have settled for too quickly.

Paradoxically, this kind of pausing saves time. Once your ideas are written down and simplified, rewriting goes quickly and flexibly.

Why active waiting is economical. In my own research projects, teachers' prewritten and prediagrammed notes that were translated into class notes took on a more casual, abbreviated form than the work of traditional lecture notes. Informal classroom notes resulted in fewer pages and took less time to write in their final form. They also encouraged more spontaneity once in class.

Teachers who talked with general points and directions in mind spent less time looking at notes, more time sustaining the attention, comprehension, and involvement of students. They even said things more directly, more simply, more memorably.

The advantages of active waiting sound too good to be true but they're not. Instead they are merely uncommon.

What usually keeps teachers from mastering these practices/ FOPs? The same thing that makes giving up impatience difficult:

issues of staying in control. The rushed intensity of impatience creates the illusion of control because we seem unstoppable and important; western civilization teaches us that displays of busyness are useful and impressive.

Consider how this sort of impatience blocks us. When we are accustomed to approaching tasks like teaching in the midst of busyness, we may feel we have too little time for preliminaries, or that we have better things to do. Even pausing for three seconds to smile at your class before beginning to speak may seem intrusive when you have lots of material to cover and you are impatient to get on with it.

Consider how simple the corrective can be. It helps to have a reminder at hand to get you to pause, such as a bold note in your classroom materials. It also helps to tell yourself, once more, the reasons why rushing undermines good teaching:

- It lowers student comprehension.

- It distances students and turns them into passive, often uncivil, class members.

- It narrows the focus and flexibility of the teacher.

- It fatigues.

Second, Pause While Working

This step resembles pausing before beginning, but it is harder. Once we are on a roll (at preparing materials or presenting them) we grow more and more reluctant to pause. Part of the problem, of course, lies with impatience.

The scenario is familiar but deserves many, many reminders: The more we rush and binge, the stronger our impatience becomes. The more we try to get everything done and said, the more we talk nonstop and discourage student questions. And, the more we attempt to impatiently do one more thing as classroom time expires, the more our students squirm.

Another reason is also about control. When we pause with a class looking at us, we can feel self-conscious and insecure. Even a pause of five seconds can seem an eternity until its practice becomes habitual. When unfilled pauses are not a familiar act, we can easily imagine that the class will instantly riot or at least conclude something is wrong. While talking nonstop appears a good way to maintain control, it isn't in most instances. We already know why from our look at

CI (classroom incivilities): When students cannot keep up with our impatient pace, when they have no respites from listening and taking notes, when they conclude we do not care about their involvement, they distance themselves from us.

Third, Use Pauses to Relax
and Contemplate but Not to Worry

Once you are practicing regular pauses (perhaps with the aid of external cues such as reminders in your notes or signals from a designated student), work more at using those interludes to calm and relax yourself. Then use them to take stock of where you are and where you will go next. The simplest versions are among the most effective:

- Slow your breathing and focus on its inward and outward flow.

- Check and readjust your posture and facial expression for more comfortable, open, and optimistic versions.

- Stretch out to loosen up. Simple Yoga postures like shrugging and holding your shoulders high as you inhale slowly, followed by a mirror-image exhalation, work nicely.

- Look at something outside the window or across the room to distance-focus and rest your eyes.

- Notice where you build tension while preparing or presenting (necks and jaws are common locations) and use pauses to relax those places (perhaps by first tensing them even more and then relaxing them).

Then, when you are learning to tolerate—even appreciate—pauses, the next step is to find better ways to ease back into your work. One kind of good transition consists of spending a moment reflecting and asking "what next?"

What, specifically, do efficient teachers do during the last, reflective parts of pauses? They look back on what they have just been doing, particularly on what worked best (while congratulating themselves on their successes). They consider whether any changes in plans are needed. And then, slowly and clearly, they quickly rehearse the next few points and how they might be said. All this fits nicely into a minute or less of reflection.

There is even time for something else important in these pauses: noticing their benefits. Without active efforts at appreciating the benefits of things like relaxing a tense jaw or knowing what to say next, active waiting may not persist long enough to become an automatic habit.

When do teachers find time for pauses that last even a minute or two? They find them right in the midst of class. They simply announce that they are taking a brief break (and that students might want to do likewise). And, despite the usual concerns of teachers, few of their students object or get out of control, and those who do soon get used to pauses and tolerate them better. More surprisingly, these interludes do not interfere with presenting enough material. In the opinion of every teacher I've seen try them beyond the point of initial discomfort, pauses help keep them on track and to the point.

What comes of active waiting, especially these first steps of pausing for calm reflection? We have already seen the payoffs in terms of increasing student involvement and decreasing teacher fatigue. These interludes of active waiting also introduce teachers to something unexpected: Pauses help change the rhythm and pacing of classroom presentations. With pauses at hand to punctuate the flow of the class, teachers begin to see that they can easily set up other rhythms. At times, for instance, they accelerate some material and slow other parts for emphasis. By changing pace, pausing, and bringing repetition into play, teachers learn to hold the attention of classes better.

As teachers become comfortable with active waiting, they are already mastering the next rule.

Begin Before Feeling Ready (Rule 3)

At first glance this third rule seems to contradict the second. In actual use it doesn't; you'll soon see why. These first-order principles won't always seem mutually consistent or even clearly separate until they become habitual practices. You *can* indeed begin early while waiting patiently; doing so is the essence of active waiting.

Beginning early generates more calm and creativity (as we saw in Chapter 2). It also helps motivate teachers more consistently. Why? Because the most reliable motivation comes in the wake of involvement in teaching. To expect motivation to appear with a cold start is to work inefficiently and unwisely. On the other hand, when teachers begin before formally beginning, so to speak, they get interested in the problem early; they make more discoveries about its nature; they experiment with ways to present it. They generate motivation in timely and reliable fashion. In contrast, teachers who hope to find motivation magically, while underway, are often disappointed.

Beginning early, before it seems you are doing the real work, also helps in another way. It propels you out of the blocks on tasks when you might otherwise hesitate and procrastinate. The earlier and more

 .ul the beginnings, the greater the chances of managing motiva-
n, imagination, and timely completions for projects. The more effi-
.ient the teacher, in my experience, the stronger the inclination to
begin early and informally.

> *Don't loaf and invite inspiration; light out after it with a club,*
> *and if you don't get it you will nonetheless get something that*
> *looks remarkably like it.*

Jack London

How Difficult Is Beginning Early?

Of course this first-order principle (FOP) isn't as easy as it sounds—at
least until it becomes an ingrained habit. Beginning early requires
patience, tolerance, and regular practice before it seems beneficial.
More important, it demands a great leap of faith. When teachers
begin early, before feeling ready, they must believe that patience and
reflection will help— even when intuition may tell them otherwise.

Because disbelief tends to be impatient, it often exaggerates the
tentativeness, imperfection, and slow pace of preliminary work.
More often, our impatience tells us that we are wasting time with
preteaching.

A Review of the Obstacles to Beginning Early

We already know these, more or less. But one of the notions behind
FOPs is that basics merit some redundancy. Here the obstacles are
restated somewhat differently:

- *Procrastination:* "I'm always behind, and I can't do things until
  the deadline is hanging over me."

- *Perfectionism:* "When I prepare or present teaching material, I
  want only my best stuff. I'd just be wasting my time on these
  vague preliminaries if they can't be the stuff I'd want my students
  or colleagues to see. For me, it's either my best or nothing at all."

- *Elitism:* "I believe that the truly brilliant teachers prepare quickly,
  in one draft of what needs saying, without having to fool around
  with preteaching, as you call it."

- *Blocking:* "Listen, teaching makes me nervous. If I think about it
  too much, I'll have an anxiety attack and not be able to present
  coherently. None of these preliminaries for me; they would make
  me a nervous wreck."

- *Freedom:* "No rules, please. I'm not a rules person, you know? If I have to use rules, I'll become too mechanical in my teaching. Spontaneity is the most important thing."

There are some striking similarities among these resistances to beginning early. In all of them, teachers want their work to be quick, easy, and unfettered (except, perhaps, by deadlines). In all of them, teachers hope that magic will provide the motivation, imagination, and structure. The outcomes of these traditional beliefs are quite different from what teachers imagine. What usually happens is that teachers who wait for magic wait passively while little that promotes good teaching takes place. They work at teaching sporadically and often feel pressured to keep up. They often struggle to get started, and they fail to appreciate the advantages of a modicum of discipline and balance:

> *The creative person is at once both naive and knowledgeable, destructive and constructive, occasionally crazier yet adamantly saner...More positively: Without knowledge, no creation; without stability no flexibility; without discipline, no freedom.*
>
> Frank Barron

You'll also recognize the other source of teachers' reluctance to begin early. Lack of trust keeps them from plunging into a bit of uncertainty. Consider the usual result of not trusting to early starts: New teachers feel insecure about their abilities to summon ideas, imagination, and patience; instead of feeling able to wait actively, novices rush ahead with what is already familiar. They put more emphasis on trying to control their emotions than on solving longer-term problems (Baumeister, Heatherton, & Tice, 1994). They fix upon a pattern that resembles a class they once took (or, just as often, one that parallels the textbook), but they do it somewhat mechanically. They imagine that getting their facts straight to avoid embarrassment is the most important thing, and they fail to think about how the material will come across. They try to have things they will say written out, word for word, (therefore increasing the possibility that "losing their place" in the notes will seem disastrous). They actually hold their breath while writing notes quickly and tensely—and will probably present them in similarly breathless fashion. Etcetera.

KNOWLEDGE GAINED FROM BEGINNING EARLY

Clearly, it seems to me, beginning early depends on the kinds of slowing and calming we saw in Rules 1 and 2. Practice of this third FOP (first-order principle) is intertwined with minimizing classroom incivilities, particularly with preparing for classes in ways that enhance our immediacy and sensitivity as teachers. All three FOPs provide more opportunity for discovery. When teachers have time to find that they know more than they thought they knew, their confidence in and openness to experimentation grow.

With proper practice teachers use preteaching sessions to collect new facts and ideas. As teachers collect and construct patiently, they grow accustomed to imagining a story line that carries students along with it. They discover how preteaching actions such as notetaking help generate efficiency.

> *Our knowledge is not just in our heads...but in accessible notes, knowing how to consult references, in having friends to call for a steer.*

> David Perkins

What efficient teachers teach often originates in the minds of students. And as teachers rely more and more on students' minds, they become better at anticipating common problems of preparation and presentation such as these (I purloined this list from a friend and hallowed pioneer of composition study, Donald Murray, 1995):

- *No territory.* There is no world of ideas, events, and personalities that the teacher and students will want to explore together.

- *No surprise.* There is no surprise in what will be said.

- *No teacher.* There is no clear individuality or personal voice in what will be presented. Students will get little sense of who the teacher is, and students learn better from and give higher ratings to teachers who reveal something of themselves.

- *Too little.* There are too many generalities, too few specifics to carry the student along in exemplary teaching, specifics follow most instances of generalities.

- *Too much.* The teacher tries to say everything she or he knows instead of picking out a few dominant themes.

- *Too private.* The content may make sense to you, but its context and meaning will not be clear to the students if it does not connect with their experience.

Of course, not all this needs mastering immediately; FOPs work by way of general acquaintance that includes patient, repeated practice. At this point, the things in the list above merely deserve watching and experimenting. One thing especially worth noticing now is how these things, if remedied, help make teaching materials more scintillating. When teachers do not pay attention to the issues just listed, they often wonder why students seem so detached from the materials presented.

This sort of noticing and planning what to notice can, of course, be practiced early with particular advantage. The "early rule" is almost always useful.

Rule 3: Begin Early, Before Feeling Ready.

PRACTICES FOR RULE 3 (BEGIN BEFORE FEELING READY)
Early starts mean what they say: beginning before feeling fully ready. They mean launching a project without having quite figured what to say. They mean letting some things, including surprises and discoveries, just happen (see Rule 2). They mean letting go in disciplined ways that generate motivation, inspiration, and connectedness. All this is easier now, as you become more patient and trusting. Practice begins, as per all FOPs, with redundancies.

First, Use Pauses in Other Activities to Think About Teaching Ideas
You can do this best when your notions of a new or revised lecture/discussion are still vague, before they seem to merit serious thought. The preliminary nature of work done this way helps keep it patient, flexible, and fun. This ensures that the work will fit these small opportunities for thinking. Its healthy combination of patience and tolerance helps keep teaching from becoming something that must always be prepared and presented in a hurry.

Carry note cards and jot down ideas and diagrams. These props encourage you to see what you could say, and how you could say things more clearly. These "external memories" also record things easily forgotten, things that can be added to or combined later.

Practice to get momentum. In my experience with teachers, pauses for playful planning become enjoyable almost immediately. Still, the pauses require regular practice for real usefulness and savings—just like any other kinds of complex intelligence. One good way to get the knack of these preliminaries is to freewrite (whatever comes to mind, without listening to your internal editors) for a minute or two about a particular class meeting or semester. Freewriting can help you get past internal censors that demand fully formed, conventional ideas. It also helps generate momentum.

Of course, there is a price to be paid for mastery of early beginnings and reflective pauses. TAs and professors who work on this strategy do indeed use some of their free moments to think about teaching and writing. They grow better and better at noticing connections between what goes on around them and their academic work. They revel in their discoveries. But they also seem more absent-minded to students and colleagues at times. That, they like to point out gleefully, is part of the academic image.

Second, Use Some Pauses Deliberately to Notice, Collect, and Connect
C. Wright Mills, the pioneering sociologist, was one of the first in the professoriate to share the secrets of what he called intellectual craftsmanship.

C. Wright Mills

This means practicing the skills of taking interpretive notes that will be useful to you later. It means taking such notes as a routine part of everyday life. Other skills follow:

- Rearrange files to look for new connections.

- Maintain an attitude of playfulness.

- Cast ideas into categories and types to help make sense of them.

    Whenever you feel strongly about events or ideas you must try not to let them pass from your mind, but instead to formulate them for your files and so doing draw out their implications, show yourself either how foolish these feelings or ideas are, or how they might be articulated into productive shape.

- Consider extremes or opposites of important ideas.

- Cross-classify to find perspectives and incongruities.

- Find comparable cases.

- Arrange the materials for classroom presentation as a way of getting yourself to bring closure, at least for the moment.

An advantage of these preteaching strategies is that you never really start "working on a project;" you are already "working" on a variety of ideas, facts, and figures, almost any of which could develop into classroom presentations. "To live in such a world," Mills liked to say, "is to know what is needed to expand, connect, or resee what you are preparing or presenting."

Third, Learn How to Decide When You Have Done Enough Preteaching for the Time Being

In a way you don't need to plan. Preteaching (beginning early, before feeling fully ready) grows into more formal acts of teaching almost imperceptibly and painlessly. What were playful preliminaries turn into a useful set of materials ready to present. But because preteaching may become more than a habit (i.e., an enjoyable act in its own right), you will generally need to pay attention to these intermediate steps to make sure they do not continue past the point of diminishing returns. I've known teachers who grew so fond of the collecting that they were hard-pressed to move beyond it to transformations that become well-summarized and organized materials for classroom presentation.

One way to keep moving ahead (albeit patiently and reflectively) is to work through sets of increasingly complete conceptual outlines. These are outgrowths of usual outlines where comments are added to each point, comments that approximate what might be said in formal prose. First versions are brief. Later revisions add detail and attend to logical flow (but ideally remain somewhat brief). For example, I started a conceptual outline for this section with this simple version.

FIGURE 1

Conceptual Outline

A. What brings patient, enduring motivation to teaching:

1. Preliminary exercises in collecting information about teaching topics from formal and informal sources (with an eye for ideas that will connect with student experience)

2. Filing and ordering and rearranging materials for classes to see simplicities and themes

3. Imagining the fun of presenting novel, connecting ideas in class

4. [and so on...]

Revised

A. What brings force/motivation to teaching:

1. A regular, casual habit of noticing and noting things that might relate to teaching enlivens my day

   ~ when I see connections to my teaching in what I read (in news accounts or scholarly pieces) or do (writing or conversing), I find myself remaining more alert, mindful, forward-looking, and optimistic.

   ~ I look forward to working out the ideas and to presenting them in class.

2. As I file, reorder, and then put ideas into revised conceptual outlines, I see ways to simplify and connect. I am surprised by things I hadn't expected

   ~ I grow more and more confident and excited about presenting the material. I find myself imagining how students will react.

3. [and so on...]

Later, in another brief pause of about 10 minutes, I picked up that still preliminary conceptual outline and quickly wrote a more detailed version. Each time I did this, I moved the process closer and closer to what I would write as prose.

How did I actually move the material along? I reordered my points to imaginarily involve you the reader as a co-journeyer who could connect and move with the story line. I envisioned which discussions and questions would involve and lead you to discoveries of your own. I coached myself to be patient and slow-moving while remaining quietly excited about the plan I am making for you and other readers. I made more notes about possible metaphors and examples I could use to explain ideas. I even drew enjoyable parallels to what I was doing at the moment (e.g., supposing that conjuring a substantive book—or lecture—is almost like planning a terrific party that brings people together for a memorable evening).

All these practices, I hope you will come to agree, work as nicely and painlessly for preparing classroom materials as for prose. Still, you might wonder about one in particular.

Benefits of conceptual outlines The format is quick and easy; preliminary versions can be done in a minute or two. Conceptual outlines help make a habit of getting fresh ideas on paper or screen, before they are forgotten or diluted. Conceptual outlines provide a quick way of controlling the material because they show the roots of its organization. They put off closure while ideas and sequences remain tentative; they encourage critiques while changes are easy and economical. And they bring repeated exposures to the material that will make classroom presentations easier and more spontaneous. So it is, as we saw earlier, that most users of conceptual outlines simply omit the final step of writing formal notes; they find they can teach more congenially and effectively with a much briefer equivalent of a conceptual outline. A final advantage is as unexpected as it is satisfying: The economies of assembling conceptual outlines usually translate into economies of presenting. Ideas are presented in simpler, more direct, more unpretentious ways. Simplicity is what first-order principles are all about.

You might still harbor doubts about how you will learn to avoid doing too much preteaching. If so, simple guidelines can help tell you when it is time to move beyond preliminaries to final copy (these points too are borrowed from Donald Murray):

It is time to move to final copy when:

- You see possibilities for teaching something you have noted and thought about.

- You have a definite, perhaps distinctive, point of view on the topic.

- You have listened to yourself prepare until you sense a "voice" in how you might present it (i.e., it will sound distinctively like you).

- What you have to says is news (e.g., somewhat novel information or a novel way of presenting it).

- You have a single line (better yet a series of points in a conceptual outline) to begin that part of the presentation, one that informs and entices students while giving you more sense of control as a teacher.

- You see a pattern in the subject, one that begins to suggest a shape for the entire piece of teaching; you begin to see and hear images (even student responses) to help guide that whole.

- You know, with some clarity, what problem you are going to solve, and you are confident you can get it said with student comprehension and discussion.

More practice. You can accomplish much the same focus and confidence by talking aloud what you might say in class to constructive listeners. Just hearing yourself talking the material helps you notice what is unclear, unconnected, unnecessary. Listener feedback will add perspectives you hadn't thought of and awareness of problems you may have difficulty seeing in yourself (e.g., too rapid a pace; too many assumptions that listeners share your context of understanding; a lack of eye contact and pauses that help connect with listeners).

Oddly, the same teachers who must sooner or later present their ideas in public to classrooms are often reluctant to practice this preliminary version. Why? They dislike having to make themselves clear before having perfected their materials. They fear that a preliminary version, one with possible mistakes, will expose them as the frauds they fear—deep down— they really are. They worry that asking colleagues to listen to a bit of a lecture plan will be an unthinkable intrusion. All these concerns are groundless in my experience. In fact, most colleagues are relieved to see that other people struggle with classroom preparations. They find these brief conversations enjoyable, despite a climate that generally discourages serious, constructive talk about teaching. And they soon reciprocate by sharing preliminary materials of their own. An important part of beginning early is making the content of teaching public, before you think it is fully worthy.

What should you do when there are not listeners readily available? Talk your ideas/plans aloud, and listen to yourself from the vantage of an imaginary audience. Better yet, tape some excerpts of what you will say and notice how clearly your organization comes across (e.g., ask, "are my transitions clearly marked and explained?") and how clear your main points are.

Fourth, Set Deadlines for Completing Preparations

The act of beginning early, like other first-order principles, thrives on economies. When preliminaries continue past the point of diminishing returns, they become procrastination. One way of knowing when you are ready to go to class with the materials in hand lies in something we saw above, in the list of cues that signal readiness. Another one was implied: Regular listeners can help tell you when you are ready.

You can attend to these few things in particular: That you've taken enough time to construct a sensible plan with sufficient supporting details and examples; that you are attending to those seven cues of readiness to present (notably an eagerness and confidence to share what you know); and that you recheck to make sure you are solving the right problem. In doing all this, a telling and liberating thing becomes apparent—patterning.

> *Everywhere one looks there is pattern, pattern, pattern. Paradoxically, only this makes behavior reasonably spontaneous. Otherwise, our familiar activities would always be as tentative and labored as our novel ones.*
>
> David Perkins

Then, as suggested by the heading comes the telling thing: A deadline. When you set clear, realistic goals for daily sessions, deadlines lose the sort of urgency they usually carry when everything must be completed by one particular date.

And when somewhat larger deadlines are added to daily plans teachers can see themselves making tangible, timely progress toward completing the whole project—all without having had teaching preparation get in the way of other important activities such as a social life, exercising, writing, and so on.

Fifth, Let Go and Take a Few Risks

This one other practice is essential to keeping deadlines in healthy fashion: You must be willing to go to class, at least once in a while, feeling imperfectly prepared. Only then, when you leave some of the details unspecified, will you be able to keep teaching preparation to a reasonable amount of time. And only then will you find real spontaneity and student involvement as you pause to think of an example (or sometimes to get students to help you conjure the connections to their own experiences).

What makes this move difficult: Concerns about staying in control and seeming all-knowing to students. Even fears that things left to spontaneity might lead to blocking (in fact they don't when preliminaries lead to broad thinking and repeated exposure to the classroom topics). Or to embarrassment. In reality, most students will *not* see these searches—your use of pauses to find examples, to clarify definitions, to restate points, to ask for help—as signs of teacher weakness. Instead, they will like the greater involvement of seeing and hearing how you solve problems. They will enjoy opportunities to help generate materials. They will appreciate the breaks in action. So will you.

Who is best at this sort of risk-taking? The most effective teachers I have studied, those who were most highly rated by students and transmitted their material most completely and understandably into student notes and explanations, were the best risk-takers. They liked the stimulation of having to figure *some* things out in class. They found that discovery kept them enthusiastic as teachers. They appreciated the value of getting the students more involved in doing some of the work. They worried far less about losing face with students and—paradoxically—were far less likely to do so.

Instead, they paid more and more attention to simplifying and improving their teaching with practices such as beginning early. Or even with strategies as strange and counterintuitive as the next one.

4

Work and Teach in Brief, Regular Sessions (Rule 4)

This fourth FOP (first-order principle) may seem most counterintuitive at first. It means preparing and presenting in brief sessions: working at classroom preparation in brief, daily sessions; and presenting materials in brief, comprehensible segments of class separated by reviews/previews and pauses). What, in all that, makes Rule 4 seem so foreign to college teachers?

Most of us binge (and enjoy it, at least in the short-run). We prepare classroom materials in great marathons that last for hours and lead to exhaustion. We present materials in one packed and hurried class meeting that barely fits the scheduled time period. More important, we chronically imagine ourselves pressed for time, always behind in what we had hoped to cover and supposing there are no opportunities for breaks or playfulness. When this happens, we cannot imagine ourselves accomplishing enough in brief sessions of work. After all, we cannot get enough done in long, grueling bouts of labor.

Despite this common predicament, though, many of the most efficient and successful teachers I have studied do almost all their work in brief sessions. They prepare for teaching in brief, daily sessions that help keep efforts unpressured, reflective, and timely. They keep teaching preps limited to durations that do not interfere with other important activities. All too often, newcomers to the professoriate spend 20-30 hours a week, or more, preparing for teaching. The results of customary bingeing include overpreparation of too much material for presentation and too little time for collegiality, scholarship, and social life.

When, in contrast, preps become a regular daily activity, they grow into pleasant habits that require no struggle to get underway. Daily habits of preparing materials also mean enhanced motivation and imagination for teaching.

Where Else Does This FOP Apply?
In class. There too you might find similar practices helpful:

- Breaking separate topics and strategies into brief segments, each with a separate identity, each related to those that precede and follow.

- Making a regular practice of setting up distinctive parts of classes: one for small talk and previews; one for discussions of each of, say, three main points for the day. Separate each of these segments by a divide in action (including, perhaps, a stretch).

What Benefits Await the Practice of this Fourth FOP?
It helps by reducing fatigue (both yours and your students') and enhancing attentiveness, merely by providing more breaks in the action and more fresh starts. It helps simplify: Each segment, because of its brevity, takes on a necessary clarity and succinctness. And, because the larger task of teaching is broken up into smaller tasks, the whole enterprise becomes easier and more timely. In that way, we can focus on the few things that need doing now.

The other advantages of brief sessions of preparing and teaching are important enough to merit this restatement.

- When teachers work daily on projects—even for just as a few minutes—ideas for classes stay fresh in mind. One result is that restarts the next day are easier. Why? We need little warm-up time to reset the context we were in the last time because it is still memorable.

- Brief, daily sessions of preparing not only help hold thoughts about teaching in mind. They also encourage sustained habits of noticing and associating in between sessions. These, in turn, cultivate imagination and creativity, not to mention motivation. Brief segments of classroom presentation (especially the pauses between them) foster noticing of links between points.

- A regular habit of working at teaching helps make the work more automatic, less of a struggle.

- Brief sessions, in and out of class, mean less fatigue.

- Brief sessions provide the unexpected benefit of relieving usual feelings that we never do enough for the day. Why? Brief sessions set clear goals for how much is enough for a day or a session—in accord with a plan to cover all the planned basics before scheduled preps or class meetings are over.

- Brief sessions necessarily provide more clarity about what gets organized and presented because short segments of work require getting to the point and using strikingly effective examples. For the same reason, they help provide teachers with more sense of control over their work.

- Brief sessions have been shown to induce better results overall. Classroom preparations are completed in far less time than with usual bingeing strategies. Preps are rated as more imaginative and memorable; materials are more likely to find their way into useful student notes. Brief sessions result in higher self- and student-ratings of the teaching and more reported sense of freedom and competence as a teacher.

So regular practice is one central kind of FOP here. Breaking the large task of teaching into manageable sub-units is another. A third may not be so obvious: For optimal persistence and expertise to occur, the work needs moderation in the doing (Rule 2). Even brief sessions can be made intense, hurried, exhausting; when they are immoderate, teachers return to old habits. Rule 4, then, relies heavily on continued practice of the other rules.

PRACTICES FOR RULE 4
(WORK AND TEACH IN BRIEF, REGULAR SESSIONS)

Practices carried over from the preceding rules get only a brief listing.

First, Use Prosocial Motivators

Commit yourself to prepare and present with an open, intimate involvement in your work. Do this in much the same way you moderate incivilities in your students: Be patient and optimistic when you can't think of something, attend to cues of fatigue and distancing in yourself and use breaks, and even briefer sessions to keep yourself on track. Put some focus on the good, the fun, the exciting in preparing and presenting; it won't hurt you to smile and be happy while assembling and imparting all that wisdom.

Second, Begin Before Feeling Fully Ready

That is, don't suppose you need motivation and certainty before getting underway; these things come more reliably once you are already working.

Third, Wait

Be patient before supposing brief sessions are inadequate to produce or cover enough material. In the meanwhile, to give Rule 4 a fair chance, practice preparing only the bare essentials and, if you must, add other things as appendices that you can cover if time permits. You won't really know if brief sessions can work until you experience them repeatedly. And if your present style of working seems rushed and stressful, what have you to lose?

With the first three rules in mind, you may be prepared to tackle the fourth and most counterintuitive of all the FOPs: Relying on brief sessions instead of long and episodic bouts of work, particularly in binges.

Fourth, Establish a Brief, Regular Time
for Preparing Classroom Materials

Prepare in the same facilitating location. Start small. If you feel too busy, too skeptical to allot, say, an hour per workday, begin with sessions of only 5–10 minutes. Part of what will prove essential is establishing a regular expectation and habit of thinking about and working at teaching on a daily basis. The other essential part is learning that you *can* accomplish a good amount and with brief sessions. Nothing in the program will seem more unbelievable at the outset; nothing will seem more obviously true and useful once it becomes a habit.

Set a regular time for working. Make yourself sit down to your notes and files, even if you do not feel like working on your preparations. At worst you will sit and stare blankly for those few minutes; at best, you will begin to freewrite, take notes, or find other ways to get going.

Arrange a regular site for writing your classroom materials. It should have few distractions (including things you would rather do, like reading the newspaper or talking on the phone). Ideally the work site will contain nothing but teaching-related stuff. And it should be comfortable, almost to the point of decadence (e.g., an easy chair that provides leg and back support). You might even want to try doing some of your preparations away from a computer screen. (Yes, you *can* still write notes and draw diagrams on paper.) There is an apparent advantage in shifting media as you translate your notes and plans to a screen version where you aim for brevity and clear organization. You might want to experiment to see what works best for you.

What keeps teachers from taking advantage of these practices? Initially, it is difficult to break (or even bend) old habits. We are not accustomed to working at teaching in small, regular bits; what had begun as a brief session might (until the new habit can compete) turn into a marathon bout where everything is finished in one sitting. Impatience to have a prep done and out of the way is a powerful temptation.

To combat that temptation, practice noticing the outcomes of brief sessions versus binges. The latter tend to require far more time than would the assembled total of brief sessions; they also produce too much material and detail to present in a way that involves students and communicates memorable points. And, just as important, binges at teaching preparation leave teachers exhausted and disinclined to take on other difficult tasks such as scholarly writing. A curious fact about working in brief, daily sessions is that it produces measurable gains in teaching and in other essential work.

We can be derailed from brief daily sessions because we imagine we don't have time for them on some days. We may be busy trying to finish other things that are overdue. We may be in a bad mood. Something unexpected may come up. Doubt about the effectiveness of brief daily sessions may reemerge, especially when we are impatient.

All these problems disappear with practice, but how can you manage even that? You might turn to a strategy you already know in other spheres, where you get yourself to do other disagreeable things (like going to a job on time) until it becomes mostly habitual.

Fifth, Force the New Habit, but Only in the Short Run

Familiar cues work: Alarm clocks, materials already set out and ready to work on without struggle, posted notes, even calls from friends to remind you it is time to get started. Will these methods be aversive? Just until the habit sets in; then they matter only on the rare occasions where you backslide.

Consider adding an even more powerful strategy. Make the cost of avoiding your scheduled brief daily sessions too expensive for most days. This means making something you would rather do contingent on first completing your brief daily session. How strong a contingency should you employ? Experiment with some that are powerful enough to ensure regular practice of brief daily sessions (e.g., earning your morning shower by first doing your daily ration of teaching preps). But do not employ contingencies that can imperil your health (e.g., earning lunch for the day and, so, supposedly benefitting yourself with weight loss if you fail to work) or social life (e.g., no calls or visits to friends for the day).

Keep contingency management flexible. Allow yourself occasional days-off for sickness or for a change of pace, particularly when you face emergencies. But keep them truly occasional (one miss per week on average). And, finally, keep the use of contingencies as brief as possible, only until the new habit is fairly reliable and automatic and enjoyable on its own. Overuse can turn them into aversions that become associated with teaching; indeed, teachers work better and more creatively in the long run by relying on internal controls. Contingencies can always be reinstated later, when the need arises, perhaps for a week or two, until you are no longer struggling to get to work on schedule.

In my experience, teachers find one kind of contingency most tolerable, most enjoyable. It consists of finding a colleague with whom to share brief daily sessions, someone they meet on a regular schedule at a good work site (e.g., the special collections room of the library). These "social contracts" work because they compel us to not let the other person down by skipping a meeting. They also enhance the process; each person sees another managing the same task and learns from that person's discoveries.

Sixth, Transfer FOPs of Brief Daily Sessions to Classrooms

Translate the first-order principles of brief, daily sessions to help divide class meetings into brief segments. When, for instance, you construct your initial preview of the day's class, plan a compelling ending that will take you into the next segment. Pause to stretch and resettle to corral tendencies to rush. And then follow the same scheme for each of the next segments: With endings that set up the next segment; with a moment for reviewing and eliciting questions; with a genuine break in the action. Depending on your preferences and the nature of the class you are teaching, you might want to experiment with segments that follow a pattern of distinctively separate coverage of:

- Small talk and preview

- Three or so main lecture sections

- Discussion periods (perhaps preceded by small group meetings where problems are solved or materials capsulized for presentation to the class)

- One-minute papers or brief daily quizzes on central concepts to check for student comprehension

- Reviews that leave time for questions and clarifications

Here, as in brief daily sessions for preparation, the likely temptation will be to persist in segments beyond planned time limits. Without brevity, it should go without saying, brief sessions cannot be brief.

Two things help deal with the usual impatience and perfectionism that impel us to try to do too much. One is the essential step of keeping the contents of each segment realistically brief during preparations (you may need some trial-and-error to determine this). The other is to prearrange cues that will tell you when time limits approach. You might enter salient reminders to check for time as you move through each of the parts of a segment (doing so also helps ensure the pauses that students so value). Or you could enlist one or more students as time-keepers to provide subtle cues (at least at first) about when time is running out. So, for example, in the second of the main lecture sections, you might want cues at two points: the halfway mark and two-minutes-to-go warning. The typical limit of such a such a section amongst experienced practitioners is about 10-12 minutes. One advantage of having materials for each section arranged in terms of minimal content is that you can cover any one of them more quickly if you have good reason to stay with another segment longer than planned. That way you can stick with the general design for the day but can take advantage of moments where you and your class have a special rapport or unexpected needs.

Here too, patience and tolerance are keys to success. Brief segments of presentation and brief daily sessions of preparation often take months of regular practice to become habitual and comfortable. Only then will you see many of their benefits:

- More sustained, imaginative involvement—yours and your students'—over a session

- More coverage of main concepts in less time overall

- Less fatigue

- Better student comprehension

If these were all the basic skills you ever acquired, you would become an outstanding teacher.

Seventh, Monitor Your Progress
To truly optimize chances of this FOP of working regularly, one more practice is important. Any kind of systematic monitoring of how well you meet your goals for brief daily sessions and brief segments will help: Graphs, charts, or journals provide feedback about how consistently you conform day-to-day. Sometimes these records indicate a need to readjust your preparations or pace. In any case, once they show consistency, records reinforce the new habit. Why? There is a surprising pleasure in watching evidence of your progress.

> *It wasn't until I kept graphs of my daily practices that I began to make real progress here. I needed to see that I wasn't being as diligent as I had imagined....When my graphs [on the level of consistency] finally went up and pretty much stayed up, I began to feel good about my progress. And I imagined that I would hate the graphing!*
> Anonymous participant in my teaching programs

Records of this sort help in another important way. They foster a readier sense of time, a surer feeling of being able to control it without rushing or bingeing. This kind of relaxed awareness of time encourages teachers to find more time to work at teaching. It enables teachers to become better noticers and listeners who change course with ease.

With all this managed, have we done enough? Yes, for the time being. But because FOPs always involve preparations for other FOPs, you might notice that you have begun to work on the next one. That is, when we manage brief daily sessions and the like with comfort, we are practicing the most difficult of FOPs, stopping in timely fashion. What had once seemed largely a problem of getting started turns out to be an even bigger challenge of stopping when you have done enough. This is so pivotal a skill that it merits a rule and a chapter all its own.

5

Stop
(Rule 5)

This rule is about timely stopping. It means stopping when you have done enough, when it is time to move on to other things. It sounds simple, but timely stopping is in fact harder and more important than starting. Why? Because timely stopping requires more effort and planning than does forced stopping. If we stop preparation sessions only when exhausted or if we end classroom meetings only when students are leaving to rush to their next classes, then we are not exhibiting timely stopping. If we cannot break the trance-like state that keeps us busy and overextended, we make the work aversive and more difficult to resume the next time.

Many of us know the usual scenario of poor stopping skills all too well. We have trouble tearing ourselves away from things we are doing before class (e.g., phone conversations). Then, when we can no longer delay, we race to class, rush to the podium, and begin lecturing without any warm up or small talk. Having dashed in, we hurry through the lecture, always trying to catch up with the overload of material we have prepared. One result is the kind of distancing we saw in the first chapter, on classroom incivilities. Another is that we tire ourselves and our students.

What Makes Timely Stopping So Difficult?

Part of the problem is a failure to make conscious precommitments. About what? Deciding how much will be enough. Noticing when diminishing returns are setting in. Leaving time to get on to next tasks without pressure and rushing.

What else typically makes this economical planning difficult? A lack of assertiveness about saying "no" to things that will overload your schedule and energy. A lack of planfulness about what is essential and what is not. Another part of the difficulty comes from the remarkable nature of momentum. Once we have impetus in hand, we dislike interrupting it. Euphoric momentum offers special appeal to teachers who are trying to do too much and who feel chronically behind in their work: It seems to provide that overdue chance to catch up at last; it tempts them to add the extra point or two that comes to mind. Euphoria offers the appearance of decisiveness and fluency; at least for the moment, we can feel we are doing something worthwhile. And for the time being, its impulsivity encourages us to believe that stopping can be put off.

Impatience and Intolerance

At a more fundamental level, these two things—impatience and intolerance—make stopping difficult. Indeed, impatience and intolerance make all the FOPs arduous at first. What have they to do with timely stopping? Quitting in the midst of something compelling demands the patience to put aside an uncompleted activity for another. Impatience tempts us to stay with the first task until it is finished, as though the opportunity to work at it again will be long in coming. What impatience overlooks is that bingeing is a vicious cycle where everything must be done in excess or not at all. Intolerance cons us into believing that stopping before feeling ready will be too painful to tolerate. And that when we do finally stop, we will no longer feel inclined to take up the next important task.

Perhaps the hardest thing about timely stopping is not doing or saying everything you could, not displaying all your possible brilliance.

> *The art of omission is hardest of all to learn, and I am weak at it yet.*
>
> Jack London

Practices for Rule 5 (Stop)

First and foremost, remember that timely stopping is proactive, not passive. And second, that it is more important than starting. Without timely stopping, there can be no timely beginnings for other things that need doing.

First, Begin to Prepare Early for Stopping, Before Feeling the Need

The easiest way to stop in timely fashion is to begin slowing and stopping early. For example, instead of leaping out of bed in the morning and resuming old patterns of mindless rushing, you might take a few moments to stretch and breathe meditatively. In that way, you will have stopped yourself from rushing while waiting and reflecting on what needs doing. Just as important, it can be a time for precommitting to the limits you will need to set up in order to have a comfortable and effective day.

For example, you might plan to spend the half-hour before going to class in relaxing, reflective ways. Many of the most revered teachers of all time have used this period to walk outdoors while reflecting on what they could say in class. You might plan to get to class 5-10 minutes early (recall from Chapter 1 the importance of establishing comfort and approachability with students). To do that, of course, requires that you stop whatever you are doing before class early. There lies the rub.

How does the same principle apply to preparations? We already know most of the answer. We can begin early by arranging materials ahead of time. When? At the ends of previous sessions. As part of preteaching and assembling materials into conceptual outlines with a few main points, as part of delimiting how much we will try to include in a class. And as part of pausing en route, we can remind ourselves of the time well before it runs short.

Second, Start on Time, but Patiently

Even while beginning classes on time, do so without being rushed or abrupt. Begin in ways that help warm up the audience: wait and smile; make a bit of small talk; briefly remind students who are barely late of what the class is doing; begin formal presentations with a review of what was done in the last meeting.

Begin brief, daily sessions of preparations just as unhurriedly and reflectively, by noticing what was done last time and what most needs doing this time.

Third, Preteach and Prewrite Briefly, Planfully, Playfully, Before Moving to the Hard Stuff

In class this "preteaching" might take the form of previewing what you plan for the day. You could give yourself and your students a broad picture of what lies ahead and a rationale for pursuing it.

Or preteaching might be seen more broadly, as, say, times during class when you step back and talk aloud your plans to change course a bit. Preteaching, in retrospect, even includes quick asides about what else you might have covered.

The most essential use of preteaching, in and out of class is, again, a matter of setting a context for your teaching. This means reminding yourself and your students where you have been and where you are going. Failure to provide context can turn otherwise well-organized information into presentations that confuse most students. Failure to set and reset context are common sources of poor student ratings for new teachers, sources that too often go unappreciated.

In brief, daily sessions for preps, use freewriting, diagraming, talking aloud, and conceptual outlines to rethink what you will prepare—even to rehearse where you are going, how it will fit together, and when you will have reached the point of diminishing returns. While doing these things, try stating contextual matters aloud to see if you are on track.

What does preteaching have to do with timely stopping? When you specify your plan in terms of clear outcomes and update your progress to yourself or your public, you are more likely to stick to essentials. When you mention what you might have said and why you are not covering it directly in class, you refrain from trying to do too much while maintaining a sense of the larger context. And when you imagine and rehearse how the points will flow and what is essential, you will prepare and go to class with clearer, more succinct material in hand. In short, when you decide what really needs doing, when you simplify what you present and plan a schedule, then stopping almost takes care of itself.

Fourth, Pause Regularly
During the Preparing and the Teaching

Pausing before stopping works for a very simple reason: pausing is itself a kind of stopping. Pausing is generally easier than completely, abruptly stopping. So pausing aids timely stopping. And pausing helps slow the pace of working from the rushed, impatient gait that makes stopping most difficult.

Pauses are already familiar in this scheme, but they deserve a few reminders about practice. In my studies of teachers in this program, pauses drop out first among the new practices of FOPs. Pauses need to be scheduled and mentally rehearsed, at least until they become strong, automatic, welcome habits, and even then they need occasional monitoring to ensure that impatience hasn't supplanted them. Pauses need to be timed as responses to telling cues: bodily tensions and discomforts such as eye strain, anxiousness, fatigue—most tellingly in mistypings and misstatements.

Fifth, Stop Most Sessions Early

This works better than planning to stop on the stroke of twelve because it leaves time for emergencies. It affords more time for student questions and contact and for reviewing context. Stopping a bit early pleases students. It encourages more reflection about the class just finished and about what needs doing to get ready for the next.

The most effective device for stopping a bit early is to stop in the middle of something—a sentence or, better yet, a whole paragraph or concept. Why? That way, the unfinished thought will remain fresh in your mind until the next time. Moreover, beginning the next time by completing what was left uncompleted makes restarting far easier than starting with an entirely new thought.

A sure way to make timely stopping more difficult is to insist on finishing everything you have to say by rushing at the last minute.

Sixth, Monitor Your Progress at Stopping Early

Start small by trying to stop only a minute or so before time officially runs out and then enter the result on a chart in your office (or wherever). As you increase the demands of this exercise (e.g., stopping early *and* in the middle of something), this record will discourage delusions about how well you manage. You may also notice something else about stopping early: it provides time to do other important things.

One more thing bears mentioning, just the sort of thing that should appear toward the end of this chapter—as I get ready to stop while feeling I could write much more on this topic. Knowing how to stop allows time to reflect on your work—a process that is better done after a session rather than during it. Why is it best to put off judging until then? Judging too soon and too harshly can prevent you from getting to the end in open-minded, happy fashion.

> *Finish, then evaluate. Perfect is the enemy of good.*
>   Donald Murray

Rule 5: Stop

6

Moderate Overattachment and Overreaction (Rule 6)

Exemplary teachers, those who work with the most efficiency and appreciation, treat teaching as important but not as urgent. They work at it regularly, playfully, and seriously, but they do not let it dominate their lives. They spend only moderate amounts of time preparing (because they keep notes informal and more focused), less overall than typical, poorly-rated, unsatisfied colleagues. Exemplars make fewer main points in class, and they convey them more patiently, with more examples and discussion. Most important, they keep some emotional distance from their teaching. The principle involved is best-known amongst writers:

The worse the writer, the greater the attachment to the writing.

What that means is that novice writers get too invested to see alternatives or to listen to criticism. It means that novices try to say too much, and they insist on saying it exactly as they planned it; they work in inflexible, inefficient, insensitive ways. The same principle applies to teaching:

> *The worse the teacher, the greater the attachment to the content.*

What Makes Moderation Difficult?

The answer is perfectionism and its secret ingredients—impatience and intolerance. Perfectionism is the enemy of moderation because moderation requires letting go of the control that underlies our overidentification with our work. Moderation, on the other hand, needs the playfulness and openness that keep us away from self-immersion and blindness to what is going on around us.

We already know why we get so attached to things we present for public scrutiny: We want them to be both perfect and admired. We don't want disapproval or indifference. Still, we know, more or less, the costs of trying too hard: rushing and premature decisions; tension, fatigue, doubts, struggles, and paralyzing anxiety; narrowness and humorless inflexibility; bingeing and difficulty stopping; and, not least, overreactions to criticism, even to indifference.

What Fosters Moderation?

Balance is the key FOP in moderating overattachment and overreaction. Balance economizes on time and fatigue. Its brevity helps teachers prepare only what needs saying and displaying and discussing (remember that one sign of expertise is presenting fewer main points but more examples of each). And, balance encourages teachers to go to class without having everything perfectly prepared: a clear, manageable scheme with some things prepared in detail, some not, suffices. Balance, with its limits on overpreparation and overattachment, is essential to several things that make teaching better: More motivated and imaginative work; more student involvement and learning; better results from less effort.

Why You Might Resist Moderation

What keeps most teachers from adopting this FOP of balance readily? For one thing, they fear the practice will cause them to lose face—to produce embarrassingly imperfect materials. For another thing, when most teachers overprepare, they are only following old customs. Status quo in higher education is hard to change. And a third thing is the skepticism teachers feel when they first encounter the balance rule. It simply seems unbelievable. "Come on now," one teacher remarked, "I can't believe that. No way you can be properly prepared for class with so little time to prepare. I know how much time it takes to prepare."

What, on the other hand, helps teachers (including the one just quoted) overcome past skepticism about balance and its greater successes? In my experience, they need to see evidence that balance works, and they need to experience the benefits of balance, particularly of letting go of complete control in favor of notes with more abstract ideas and plans than details about what, exactly, they will say. Three experiences seem especially crucial:

- The joy of being able to prepare exciting, imaginative classroom materials in brief, daily sessions

- The blending of excitement with patience so that clarity dominates

- The satisfaction of working, in the long run, with more efficiency, even more useful control

Many teachers link these incidents with "flow."

> *Although flow appears effortless, it requires highly disciplined mental activity....jobs are easier to enjoy than free time because, like flow activities, they have built-in goals, feedback, rules, and challenges...all of which encourage concentration and losing oneself in work.*
>
> Mihaly Csikszentmihalyi

A fourth experience is also essential:

- Without regular practice at moderating our reactiveness to disapproval and criticism, we will make not make much progress with balance

Why is the fourth point true? In my research projects, only the ingrained habits of patience and tolerance for the rejections and rudeness all of us encounter will keep us from teaching defensively. Without regular practice at balance, we will be tempted to continue to overprepare ("at least that way, no one can accuse me of not knowing my material"), to work too hard to remain in control of class ("I keep busy writing on the board and presenting lots and lots of good material; no one can say I'm not working hard"), and to be surprised at the comments of some student malcontents ("I can't believe that people wrote that I am intimidating and unfriendly").

Together, these FOPs about moderating overattachment and overreaction suggest the following moves:

PRACTICES FOR RULE 6 (MODERATE OVERATTACHMENT TO CONTENT AND OVERREACTIONS TO CRITICISM)

This rule initially proves difficult and counterintuitive. It is a lesson in modesty and humility—no easy matter for academics, including me. The assignment is particularly difficult for newcomers to the professoriate who suppose they must, first and foremost, never lose face. Of course, it turns out that trying too hard to save face is an invitation to losing it; exemplars take more of the risks outlined below and experience far fewer embarrassments than do counterparts.

Why are modesty and good-natured humility uncommon amongst college teachers? Too few of us, I think, have been taught to laugh at ourselves, our pretensions, or our work. Fewer still know how to learn from criticisms. Even so, moderation is not all that difficult to attain.

First, Monitor for Overattachment

This is the most basic step. Its practice can seem deceptively simple. During pauses—both in and out of the classroom—watch for signs that you are not keeping your distance and playfulness. These are the tell-tale clues:

- A pronounced reluctance to stop because your writing or teaching seem too brilliant to interrupt

- Feelings, early on, that your work must be superior to that of most teachers and that it must, therefore, be perfect and impeccable

- A reluctance to share your preliminary plans/preparations for fear that colleagues will either steal or undervalue your ideas

- A growing anticipation that your presentation will be so deep and complex that only the brightest, most deserving students will appreciate it

- A diminishing sense of joyfulness and humor about your work (e.g., notice: are you and your students frowning tensely and/or distantly apathetic?)

- An urgency to finish all of the planned content

Of course, these feelings are not always inappropriate. Even exemplars have moments where they are impressively perfect and cleverly insightful. The key, again, is balance. The problem arises when perfectionistic feelings are so commonplace that you are disproportionately overattached to all your work. The solution begins with a bit of modesty. Recognize that not every moment of your presentations needs to be so perfect that you wouldn't want to change it in another go-around. That you need not be captivating every minute (indeed, students fare better with changes of pace, some calming, some exciting, some downright dull). That the more important goals are to manage clarity, to watch and maneuver for comprehension, and to have a good time (yes, even in our Puritanical culture).

Second, Encourage Criticism, the Earlier the Better

This brave act, like so many practices of patience and tolerance, begins with proactiveness. In contrast, most teachers I have studied are passive about criticism: They wait for critics to come to them after class (this produces an unrepresentative sample of student opinion, too much of it from ingratiators or whiners). They ask, rather weakly, for complaints and suggestions in classes, but most students are too shy to say anything substantial in such settings. And they rely on formal student evaluations (usually administered at semesters' ends and fed back months later) to learn what might need changing, far after the fact. Curiously, these same teachers remain impatient for obvious signs of student approval.

A little-appreciated fact about teachers who struggle is that they work too privately, with too little feedback. They prepare alone, without discussing their plans and ideas. Their colleagues rarely visit their classes or learn much about what gets taught in them. And their students, most of them at least, remain anonymous transients. Years later these teachers cannot tell you much about their students and their students can recall only the barest notions of what the class was about ("All I can remember is that he was a sharp dresser"). Why? Teachers who remain passive about getting early feedback learn too little, too late about how best to change or about what their students are like.

Third, Practice Tolerance and Patience in Response to Criticism

Efficient, effective strategies are more public and more open. And when teaching is responsive to ongoing criticism, it is far more successful in the long run. In the short run, though, practices of tolerance and patience with critics can be almost unbearably painful. The following strategies can help you progress somewhat gradually toward the most difficult parts:

Ask critics, beforehand, to limit their comments to only a few things that you yourself wonder about. For example, "Do you see anything missing from this list?", and other inquiries where you know you will probably not be hurt by the response. With practice, move to slightly riskier questions (e.g., "Can you think of a better opening point than mine?"; "Was I making good eye contact?"). Like any other kind of phobia, dislike for criticism is best moderated by way of what psychologists call exposure therapy: becoming more comfortable with something through repeated exposures to or with it.

Ask critics to make comments specific in terms of what you might need to do to render your preparations and presentations better. This means not accepting vague criticisms (e.g., "Your presentation was unclear"). It means calmly asking for more specifics ("OK, please tell me what I should do to make it clearer"). And, as you muster more bravery, it means asking critics to begin with specific and positive comments about at least one thing you have done well— despite the proud tradition in academe of sticking solely to criticism. In actual practice, few critics refuse this request or even see it as an imposition. They may simply be unaccustomed to doing it.

Find ways to stay relatively calm and nonreactive while learning about your criticism. If you expect a strong response, get it by way of an intermediary who restates the critic's remarks or written comments in gradual, tactful fashion. In that way, you will be better able to sort the useful message from what might seem intolerably personal and hurtful. In that way, you can expose yourself to criticism more slowly and more tolerably. Then, when you are ready to hear or read critics directly, maintain your calm, open focus by taking careful notes on what needs doing differently. Stop your critic, calmly, for clarification if necessary. Doing this can also defuse what would otherwise be a tense situation.

Practice ways of agreeing with criticism, at least some aspect of it. Begin by recognizing a basic truth about teaching efficiently: All critics, even the harshest or most ill-informed, have something worthwhile to teach us. If the critic hasn't even listened carefully, find out what put him or her off from a closer and more patient look. If your critic has misunderstood your message, investigate to see where the confusion occurs. If your reader/listener is offended, inquire about the stimulus. It may be something minor that you hadn't noticed such as too fast a pace; it may be something major, like a sexist comment.

An especially effective strategy for doing these counterintuitive, unfamiliar things is to begin your spoken or written response by finding something with which you can honestly agree (e.g., "I can understand how some people might not find this interesting, but..."). Thank your reviewer for her/his work (reviewers are rarely paid or properly appreciated). Request clarification of what needs doing differently or better. And then enlist critics early in the teaching process, the earlier and more systematically the better (during preparations; in early lectures).

Still other ways of economizing on reactions to criticism can be experienced in the next few rules and chapters.

7

Moderate Negative Thinking and Strong Emotions (Rule 7)

One other way we can moderate overreactions and overattachments is to reduce negative thinking and excessive emotions as teachers. In a sense, we have already been practicing these restraints by way of calming and slowing for reflection (Rule 2) and stopping in timely fashion (Rule 5). This seventh rule, though, adds a stronger psychological component. It means noticing the thoughts, attitudes, and feelings that get in the way of effective teaching.

I start with the thoughts that accompany teaching and move to the emotions after that. Ultimately, these practices of self-control deal with thoughts and emotions more interactively.

How Does Negative Thinking Impact Teaching?

Most of us know the answer all too well, once we pause to notice. When we think perfectionistically, we place unrealistic demands on ourselves to cover everything and to make no mistakes. When we think anxiously, we put off preparations rather than face the distant prospect of apathetic and rejecting students. When we listen to our internal censors, we avoid even the smallest risks; instead, we narrow our attention to concerns about losing our place in our notes or saying something with which someone might disagree.

Then: We think of teaching as difficult and unrewarding (no wonder, given the discomforts our self-talk is creating for us). We rush preparations and presentations and, horror of horrors, we lose our places (and, seemingly, our faces) as we stumble and grow more and more worried.

Negative thinking exacts even greater prices. Its pessimism and helplessness set the stage for depression and its inaction (or overreaction). Its excessive self-focus keeps us shy and isolated, apparently unapproachable and aloof, definitely unable to find or accept social support or affection. Its self-criticism (and that is what most negative thinking is) inclines us to expect failures and to give up prematurely. And its impulsivity (with roots in the impatience and anger that underlie negative thinking), makes patience with ourselves and our students all the more difficult. The more impulsive we are, the more we opt for the quick, the easy, and the immediately relieving. The result is a less than ideal condition for creativity or happiness in the long run.

> *Pessimists are at the mercy of reality.*
> Martin Seligman

How Can You Tell When Your Thinking Is Getting in the Way of Your Teaching?

By noticing when it is constantly focused on future or past events, on anxieties and regrets (and not on the present moment, especially the task at hand). By noticing when it delays and discourages and discomfits (and makes you want to do something other than teach). By noticing when it leads to overreactions. And, by practicing the strategies outlined below:

PRACTICES FOR RULE 7 (MODERATE NEGATIVE THINKING)

Correctives for negative thinking are not difficult, even if you imagine yourself totally unqualified to practice psychology. Practical solutions appear in a variety of best-selling books that make self-therapists of readers (e.g., Seligman's *Learned Optimism*; Ellis & Knaus' *Overcoming Procrastination*). Strategies that work best in my programs for teachers are among the simplest of these.

First, Habitually Monitor Your Thinking During Preparations and Presentations

This is easy but not as easy as it sounds; most of us are unaccustomed to noticing the nearly constant self-talk that goes on in the backs of our minds. While much of it ordinarily goes unheard by the conscious self, it can nonetheless undermine what we try to do.

The key words to becoming a useful observer of negative thinking are the usual pair—patience and tolerance: Patience to keep watching and listening, even when nothing seems to be there; tolerance to hear the amazingly negative, depressing, irrational things we often say to ourselves.

Begin by noticing (and noting) your self-talk at just one critical time, the few minutes that precede the beginning of a brief daily session for preparing or the walk to class. Are you worrying about needing to do something other than the task at hand (e.g., answering your mail)? Are you fretting about getting caught up on overdue work or about teaching perfectly? Do you anticipate failures and embarrassments, and do you dwell on past disappointments? Have you convinced yourself you are not in the mood, that you need more time to clarify thinking or to look up even more references before you start preparing? Do you tell yourself to make up for your dissatisfaction by attempting one more thing (a supposedly quick phone call) before heading off for class at what could have been a leisurely pace? Are you still ruminating over a social slight or an argument that keeps you from concentrating? The list could go on and on, but you see the point. These are thoughts well worth noticing and arresting.

Second, Dispute Negative Thinking

This, too, takes regular practice, but not much. It requires noticing and challenging the usual absurdity and deception of negative thinking by consciously, mindfully listening to how rational the thought is when it is repeated slowly. If, for instance, you find yourself imagining that your teaching surely will be criticized or rejected (perhaps even that grading tests or papers is drudgery and should be put off for the time being) consider this: A bit of reflection exposes the irrationality in supposing that *all* our classroom comments will be disparaged or that we will fare better by putting off tasks until we must rush (and dislike) them. This kind of awareness of irrational thoughts helps move teaching beyond its usually mindless, inefficient beginnings.

The main skill of optimistic thinking is disputing. This is a skill everyone has, but we normally use it only when others accuse us wrongly....You can, with some discipline, learn to become a superb disputer of pessimistic thoughts....Once you are good at doing it, it makes you feel better instantly.

Martin Seligman

Third, Replace Negativities with Constructive, Optimistic Thinking

When you have disputed and dismissed an irrationality, turn your thinking to getting on with the task (e.g., "Once I'm doing the teaching, I'll enjoy it. I might just as well go and do it and enjoy it; it only lasts 80 minutes").

The essence of this third step is moving away from *product* orientations to *process* modes of working. Product orientations look too soon at outcomes, long before there are any. They induce pressures about working fast enough and with perfectionism that can only make teaching more difficult than it needs to be. They take the joy out of the moment.

Process styles, in contrast, are more practical and efficient. They focus attention on the present, on how to make the process of preparing and presenting comfortable and fluent. Process modes bring a letting-go of regrets about the past and of anxieties about the future; both of which can distract us from working patiently and reflectively. With regular practice at process modes of noticing and replacing irrational thoughts, teachers learn to get themselves on track with a simple reminder like this: "Just do it."

In the longer run, these strategies lead to deeper changes. Teachers discover the inefficiency of pessimism and the efficiency of optimism. That is, they learn to reinterpret the things that happen in a more positive light (e.g., by supposing that failures do not reflect a massive personal weakness but, rather, a correctable problem such as preparing ineffectively). With this greater awareness of the process of teaching, something else happens. Teachers pay more attention to pacing, to rates of output and levels of quality, to sustaining discoveries, and to the joys of working without a background of tense, negative thinking.

Remember this about teaching: Whenever you find yourself and/or your class reacting negatively, pause to look at and talk about the process. You might notice that you are feeling angry toward a few disrespectful students and letting your overreaction affect your treatment of everyone (as opposed to the more efficient act of addressing the specific incivility). You might see that a controversial topic you brought up is leading to emotional interchanges that overwhelm the class (a better process might include resetting the context and ground rules for conversation). It is almost never hurts to pause to look at both kinds of processes as you teach: the one internal, in your own mind, and one external, in the class.

Practices for Rule 7 (Moderate strong emotions)
Some parts of the problem of excessive emotions in teaching might be obvious. Preparing or presenting without emotion leads to dull experiences, weak motivation, missed communication. Teaching with too much emotion (say, anger or sustained excitement) can distance students who, in turn, feel too alienated or rushed to remain involved. Excessive emotions exhaust teachers.

Q: What helps bring moderation to teaching?

A: Preteaching strategies that generate excitement combined with patient discovery. Practice at pausing and stopping.

Q: And what generally obstructs those FOPs?

A: The excitement and decisiveness generated by rushing.

To Understand the Problem of Rushing
We Need to Look at One of Its Extreme States
Hypomania (i.e., a near-state of mania) is a pathological circumstance that comes with prolonged rushing and emotional escalation. Its short-term benefits are tempting (and often addictive), but its long-term costs far outweigh them. True, bingeing at teaching brings an enchanting euphoria, even a seeming creativity and charm (e.g., recall stories about teachers who never miss a beat as they keep on talking while letting late students in the door). But all these notions are largely illusions.

The problem with hypomania goes beyond the superficial and disorganized writing/talking it often produces. Even beyond the exhaustion that makes starting again difficult. Hypomania commonly leads to dysphoria (just as mania begets depression) and its sad inaction. With this cycle in place, teachers work at preparations only sporadically and at teaching mostly fretfully, reluctantly. When they at last break out of their depressiveness, they work up the emotional state that ensures the opposite experience—hypomania. And when they have exhausted themselves in a binge, they are predisposed to another bout of dysphoria. Not only does hypomania make working unreliable and inefficient; it also produces mood swings that interfere with everyday living. In fact, hypomania produces a measurable wake of depression, it reduces the output and quality of teaching in the long run, and it makes teaching seem more difficult. It even undermines the health and social relations of teachers.

All This Does Not Mean that Hypomania Has No Place in Efficient, Effective teaching

Moderation includes flexibility. Balance includes some time spent in excitement. Teachers who write and present with the most fluency and happiness generally keep working emotions at low to mid-range levels. At the same time, though, they are aware of the value of changing their pace occasionally. Sometimes they use a burst of excitement to work past their internal censors or to convey the appropriate voice in their writing or presenting. Other times they prepare dispassionately (just to get ideas down on screen or paper), knowing they can wait to find more imagination in revising it later. On occasions that they and others judge as their best work, they display a rhythm based in mild happiness, one punctuated by occasional swings in mood that do not persist to the point that impedes returning to base level.

PRACTICES FOR RULE 7 (MANAGE EMOTIONS)

At this stage of my programs, teachers become close observers of their moods (to notice which impede or impel working, to see how they relate to thinking). And here teachers become patient experimenters who compare the effects of working under hypomania versus moderation.

First, Monitor and Record Mood Levels and Types During Prep Sessions

Begin by rating your working emotions in a continuum with, say, high nervous tension at one end and serenity at the other. That emotional domain might be labeled anxiety/fearfulness. With practice at noticing affective states as simple as happiness while working (something most of us have not been trained to do), other emotions such as anger, fear, or anxiousness will become apparent. Aim for awareness of how all these emotions affect writing, speaking, interacting.

It takes a few months, in my experience, for teachers to become decent observers of their working emotions.

Second, Set Reasonable Goals for Emotional Management

At the least, try to instill and maintain the calm pacing you already know about. Then add the emotion of mild happiness to it. Why? Both optimize the kinds of problem solving essential to preparing and presenting. Both make teaching more enjoyable and rewarding.

How can you tell if you are calm and mildly happy? Stop and observe; compare your feelings and expressions with occasions when you were undoubtedly so.

How can you induce these states if they are not there? Scan for negative thinking and supplant it with positive thoughts. Plant a faint smile on your face (this grows easier with practice, even for the New Yorkers I work with), but not the fixed sort displayed by beauty contestants. Recall, for the moment, a pleasant, calming experience such as sitting near a waterfall with fragrant ferns smelling of sunlight. And, with practice, notice the components of pleasant emotions such as joy.

> *Joy is sensed as pleasant, desirable, feeling…comfort and well-being and relaxation, even playfulness…movements seem easier, accomplished by strength and vigor and openness and receptivity and creativity.*
>
> Carroll Izard

Expect to struggle, at least at first, in the absence of usual tension. Until then, you might suppose, mistakenly, that you are not working hard enough (or suffering enough). In the longer run, anticipate something else surprising. Successful teachers work with only a low but noticeable level of emotions as a rule. But they also rely on changes of pace to keep them going.

Third, Work with a Sense of Rhythm

This seemingly foreign, mysterious skill (rhythm in teaching) begins, as we saw much earlier, with the simple acts of pausing and stopping in timely fashion. Those are the hardest parts. With them comes more awareness of when it is necessary to slow down to get ready to stop. And with that grows a greater appreciation that writing and talking can be done at differing paces—and of how changes in gait (and their emotional states) affect your work. Sometimes, you might find benefit in writing as deliberately as though you are doing calligraphy or speaking to a non-native speaker of English, crafting succinct, clear sentences. Sometimes you might look to add elements of repetition or parallel (as with the "sometimes" just above and below) to induce elementary rhythm in speaking. Sometimes you might ensure a steady pace by working (even teaching) in concert with your becalmed breathing. Sometimes you might make a contrasting point or add a short sentence to change the pace. And other times you might simply pause to savor something you have just done well. Learning to work efficiently at teaching is in part a matter of learning to enjoy its highlights and variations:

> *Vary your discourse; a style too equal and uniform puts us to sleep....Keep a sharp ear for the cadence of your words.*
>
> Boileau

Learning to enjoy teaching is also about appreciating the nature of its most rewarding emotional states.

Rule 7: Moderate Negative Thinking and Strong Emotions

8

Let Others Do Some of the Work (Rule 8)

This may be the most counterintuitive of all the rules about letting go of control. Still the fact is that efficient, respected teachers excel at letting other people do some of the work. They, compared to most teachers, collaborate more often, sharing the work of presenting in classes. Efficient teachers encourage more observation and criticism of their work, even early in the planning process. Efficient teachers learn a sense of audience that includes joining ongoing conversations.

Traditional Misbeliefs About Working Alone

Teachers often resist the general move advocated in Rule 8. Why? Our society credits special genius to artists, inventors, writers, and teachers who seem to work alone. It perpetuates myths about writers and teachers who apparently produce finished, flawless work in a flash of brilliance, without any obvious preparation or notes. It encourages beliefs that ideas and materials shared early, while still imperfect, will create irreversibly negative images in our readers and students. It holds that asking for help is always an imposition. And it condones the belief that good writing and brilliant teaching are completely original.

Graduate students and professors caught up in these mistaken beliefs are likely to suppose that letting others do some of the work is tantamount to weakness or manipulation. Said one newcomer to me: "If it isn't all mine, all my own work, why bother?" Said another: "You have to understand that I value my autonomy above everything else. No way am I going to ask for help." And another: "I can't impose on busy, successful people" (even while admitting that she would welcome requests for feedback from other teachers).

The efficient teacher not only delegates some of the responsibility, as any good manager does. S/he also cheerfully admits that most writing and teaching is borrowing and restating of old ideas; there is nothing new under the sun. Efficient teachers actually take joy in sharing the credit for collaboration and assistance. They know that appropriating other people's ideas but restating them and putting them into different contexts is not plagiarizing (particularly when mentioning sources). They know that soliciting early critiques and suggestions for change does not constitute shirking (even in school settings where things like term papers and dissertations are traditionally not shown to anyone until seemingly finished and perfect). They particularly take advantage of other writers and teachers by studying their modes of description and rhythm, adapting what they like to their own work. By interacting with other writers and teachers, as critics and as beneficiaries, they learn more about the FOPs of working.

An already familiar example may help make the point. Teachers who dominate classrooms by doing all the talking not only work harder than they need to; they also deny students sufficient involvement in discussions. And they limit the learning that goes on, the approval ratings that students give, and the satisfaction of teaching that comes with real intimacy and connectedness.

PRACTICES FOR RULE 8
(LET OTHERS DO SOME OF THE WORK)

Involving others means letting go of some of the control and credit for teaching. Curiously, it also helps make teaching more public and more publicly acceptable. Surprisingly, it is the most difficult of social skills for teachers, one commonly overlooked and underappreciated. Once more, efficient teachers suggest solutions.

First, Establish Social Contracts
to Stay on Schedule for Preparations

We saw this practice in a preliminary way as part of Rule 4, while setting contingencies to impel the habit of brief sessions of working. Here, in the eighth rule, that act grows broader, to finding a regular partner who will listen to parts of what you are writing and diagraming for the day (and you to his/hers). Why does this help? Simply knowing you will read what you plan or write helps bring focus and clarity to your work. Actually reading it and hearing it suggests better ways of communicating it. And having someone else stop you for clarifications and other comments helps make teaching more efficient.

In similar fashion, enlist a friend or two to exchange working materials at regular intervals. There is no necessary reason why teaching preparations must be done in isolation. This social contract helps ensure timely completion of at least some material, and it provides hints of the kinds of criticisms and misunderstandings likely from students after it is presented for public scrutiny. More important, a social style of preparing helps generate an excitement of shared ideas and discoveries even before class gets underway.

With the aid of this early and ongoing feedback, teachers are more likely to make changes. With the gentle, repeated suggestions of where listeners will react badly, they grow habituated to the criticisms that lie, inevitably, down the road.

These social partnerships seem to work best when teachers can carry somewhat parallel projects from beginning to end. In this way, both of you will be prompted to put your ideas for classes outside your minds and into speech and then onto paper or screen. The sooner you begin to work out your ideas in conversations and in writing, the more quickly your preparations will proceed. Much of the important work that others can do for you is to get you to externalize your ideas and plans, the earlier (and more regularly) the better.

Second, Collaborate in Classroom Teaching,
at Least Occasionally

Some co-teachers are disappointing because they don't communicate well. But more of them provide educational experiences that cannot be had elsewhere. Shop around. Close, interactive planning provides a rare opportunity to discover how other teachers think and work. Collaboration during classes (i.e., turn-taking at speaking) can bring a richness of combined styles and ideas that no one teacher could have conjured. Collaboration even reduces the kinds of oversights and miscommunications that undermine public acceptance. And it can produce a completed preparation and presentation in far less time than if done solo.

Third, Observe and Critique Others' Classes

When you analyze the teaching of colleagues, you learn a lot about becoming a better teacher in your own classes. Sometimes you will see things to emulate, sometimes things to avoid.

Fourth, Join the Conversation

All these are exercises in letting others do some of the work and in moving away from the solitude and autonomy that traditional teachers have claimed to prefer. And all of the practices, done well, amount to making work at teaching more social. That includes more than just sharing as you prepare. It also means socializing with other teachers working on courses like your own. It means recognizing that when you teach in a new area, you become part of an ongoing conversation carried out by colleagues in other classrooms and on other campuses. As in any social conversation, if you speak out in the group without first having listened to what others have been saying, you will be naive. If you listen to how others are posing problems, you can reshape your contribution while, nonetheless, making sure you have something relatively new and interesting to add.

To the extent that you learn from the conversation (e.g., how to state problems; how to present arguments, how to formulate creative ideas), you let others do some of the work. Successful teaching isn't only a matter of learning how to produce good classroom material in timely ways. It is just as much a skill of accepting help from others, even competitors and critics.

An analogue, from writing again, helps make the last strategy more concrete. When we submit brief conceptual outlines to editors early, we can save ourselves a lot of work by asking little more than "Does this seem to be on track, the sort of thing you are looking for?" Socially skilled writers work efficiently by discovering if they are solving the right problem before they get too far along to make changing their course expensive. (Imagine the inefficiency of the alternative—waiting until the manuscript is finished to discover that your work is off-track.) By presenting editors with such a simple plan, you encourage information from these experts about points and directions you have missed. You get them invested in your success. The problem with this suggestion, in my experience, is that writers commonly suppose such a request will be seen as an imposition or display of weakness. In fact, most editors I have queried prefer to see manuscript ideas early, when they can still be redirected with ease. These gatekeepers, in my experience, will tell you this: They particularly dislike having to criticize, reject, or fail writing that reflects hard work but unacceptable content.

The principles apply, so far as I can tell, to teachers. The earlier they share ideas for teaching with critics, the better.

A CAUTION NEAR THE END OF THESE RULES

Our reservations must still be given their due. Some writers and teachers proceed through these rules more slowly and skeptically than others. Some are more timid about trying new strategies. Why?

> *Publication—is the auction of the Mind of Man.*
> Emily Dickinson

So too, teaching.

Almost all teachers I have known tailor these rules to fit their own personalities and needs. Some take risks more happily than others. The commonality underlying these individual differences is this: Those who "let go" most readily find the most productivity and acceptance.

Moderation takes on surprising faces. Some of the teachers who have displayed the greatest success with these rules like to add this spontaneous comment as they develop more and more expertise:
The worse the participant, the greater the attachment to these rules.

Rule 8: Let Others Do Some of the Work

9

Welcome Learning and Change (Rule 9)

Most of us begin by assuming ourselves to be already expert as teachers. We imagine we need only ideal circumstances (e.g., adequately prepared students; the right course topic) to display our true brilliance. Or, we imagine we merely need a few bits of advice and some seasoning to master teaching. As a result of all these stances, we do not see ourselves as needing to learn much to teach well (and, more likely, we may be only vaguely aware that resources for learning to teach exist).

Origins of Usual Beliefs About Teaching

While these attitudes toward teaching are rarely examined closely, their sources are easily understood. For one thing, most of the professoriate treats teaching lightly—as something that needs little coaching or attention. (And then we reward it accordingly.) We train our graduate students extensively in areas of content and research, usually not at all in teaching skills. We assume that anyone who knows the subject area can teach well enough (and that anything more might be pandering to students). We even suppose, some of us, that too much encouragement for teaching will undermine scholarship and research. And, in the main, we leave the heaviest teaching loads for colleagues who fail to get jobs at prestigious universities or who do not publish much.

None of this is news. But we may not have stopped to reflect on what this cultural ethic does to us as teachers. It leaves most higher educators in the position of never having learned to teach efficaciously or rewardingly. It helps keep teaching in the position of something to be avoided or treated as superficially as possible. It turns many faculty members into creative dodgers of teaching who will do almost anything (even administration) instead. It helps keep most university teaching, especially of undergraduates, in an increasingly dismal state. And, most important, it deprives many of us of the unique experience of learning how to teach well enough so that we change the ways we think, communicate, and find satisfaction as professors.

Why Wait Until Now to Bring This Up?

In my experience, most novice teachers are disinclined to welcome learning about teaching in a broad sense until they have gotten to this point. Patience and tolerance leave all of us more open and congenial to learning about something that, initially, seems counterintuitive and counter-cultural. By this juncture in my programs, participants show a ready interest in exploring the literature on teaching. First-order principles make understanding and mastering the higher-order principles of such books and articles easier—even pleasurable. Teachers with patience and tolerance not only find joy in teaching; they look for useful sources of expertise that can make their teaching even better.

If you haven't already acquired this habit of investing some scholarship in teaching, I recommend you begin by reading and discussing a sampling of classics in the field. As usual, I offer my advice in the form of structured practices (always expecting you to modify them to suit your tastes).

PRACTICES FOR RULE 9
(WELCOME LEARNING AND CHANGE)

I overview two classics as a stimulus to get you moving beyond this presentation of FOPs to everyday practice in teaching. Both of these books reward direct reading. Together they represent only a small part of an enormously rich literature, in books and journals, that has too long been overlooked by the professoriate. Each includes hints of what we are calling FOPs; much of the best advice for teachers is basic.

Here I overview the two books in fleeting fashion, with just enough details, I hope, to stimulate you to read more.

The first is the all-time classic book of advice for novice teachers, one that long ago made the world, or most of it, forget early staples such as William James' *Talks to Teachers* (1899).

McKeachie, W.J. (1994). *Teaching Tips*, 9/e. Lexington, MA: D.C. Heath.

Teaching Tips has achieved multiple editions because it is readable, upbeat, and useful. It aims, specifically, to help new teachers find effective, comfortable beginnings. It assumes that teachers who have discouraging beginnings may be handicapped for life. And it emphasizes a variety of attractive strategies for establishing friendly communication with students, even those who start out in unruly ways. In the main, then, its premises are much like those here, in *First-Order Principles of College Teaching*.

The difference, I think, is that *Teaching Tips* operates in a different way. On the one hand, it excels at providing advice for almost any contingency, and it does so in reassuring ways. But its advice is either too general (e.g., imploring readers to build their abilities to manage the activities of their classes effectively) or else too specific (e.g., "A…surprisingly effective device is to have each person introduce everyone who was introduced before, ending with the teacher repeating everyone's names") to generate the kinds of simple rules I favor (i.e., FOPs). I suspect, from listening to the reactions of many new readers who have read *Teaching Tips* and *First-Order Principles* that there is a special benefit in reading both, particularly in seeing how McKeachie's tips can be linked to FOPs and in recognizing how FOPs can be appreciated in broader, more practical ways.

So, for example, where I address matters of establishing good work habits and preteaching materials early, *Teaching Tips* speaks more directly to specifics (e.g., begin preparing three months early by writing down your course objectives; aim for a base of concepts and skills that will facilitate further learning and thinking; and draft a syllabus that will force you to plan what will fit and what will not. Then, two months early, plan assignments—keeping in mind what you want students to learn from the course; making sure you assign suitable amounts to various topics; and choosing an appropriate teaching method such as combined lectures and small group discussions).

McKeachie is renowned for his advice about getting discussions underway in classes. He advises starting them with a common experience or even a controversy; he describes ways of engaging nonparticipants by having everyone write down first approximations to answers (and then having some students read their answers). He outlines ways of handling discussion-monopolizers by having them act as observers who keep records of student participation, and, as a last resort, by talking to verbose students outside class.

And he goes on to provide his usually succinct counsel about lecturing, testing, grading, dealing with diverse students, etc.

Restated, then, what makes *Teaching Tips* different from my own book on FOPs? Mostly the FOPs about learning how to work (e.g., calming and slowing and pacing). Fans of McKeachie's book (and there are many) could legitimately argue that following his tips can eventually produce many of the same results. But I would argue, in friendly fashion, that learning FOPs before mastering McKeachie's tips makes the overall process quicker and more democratic (indeed, research shows just that—Boice, 1995a). And that, in the long run, patience and tolerance are the most important things excellent teachers learn.

I have also tested the effects of first practicing FOPs before trying the practical advice in another leading book. Maryellen Weimer's beloved guide for teachers is also "must reading," in my view.

Weimer, M. (1990). *Improving College Teaching*.
San Francisco, CA: Jossey-Bass.
This book, like McKeachie's, reflects the personality of a writer who is cheerful but practical about teaching. Her initial point is worth remembering: College teachers receive too little training and, so, perpetuate many misbeliefs about teaching, notably the one that says "if you know it, you can teach it." As a result, most college teachers suppose they need learn little more than content.

This premise, about the worth of raising teachers' consciousness to include improvement in process matters of teaching (e.g., the actual skills of teaching in ways that effect student learning) is rather like my own on FOPs. We are both saying, more-or-less, that it is as important to learn how to work as a teacher as it is to become expert in subject matter.

What Weimer adds to my emphasis on basics, I think, are things like these: New teachers need to become aware of how well they really teach (by way of impressively specific and useful feedback devices) and how well they could teach (while realizing that without this awareness, teaching becomes psychologically and emotionally draining). An essential part of learning to teach is facing interconnected realities: ever changing student populations and ever more diverse students who require diverse teaching methods for success. And, not least, that most of us will feel threatened when our teaching is examined and improvements are proposed (because the need to improve presumably denotes incompetence in the very areas where we see ourselves expert).

Specifically, Weimer outlines five steps (each of them with FOP-like properties) for teachers who want to improve:

1. Develop instructional awareness about what you do when you teach (e.g., use behaviorally-orientated checklists to foster a sense of details that comprise teaching).

2. Gather information about how well you really teach (e.g., have classroom observers notice how you affected them).

3. Make choices about changes about how to improve, based in part on your observers' hunches (e.g., ways to enliven a point in your lectures or discussions).

4. Implement the alterations, incrementally, by way of trial and error.

5. Assess the alterations.

How will you know when you are making significant gains? You have, at last, gotten yourself to see teaching as an endeavor in its own right, not as something subsumed within your content knowledge, by focusing attention on the essential processes and behaviors of teaching.

Closing Suggestions About How to Implement These Two Resources

These two examples of the traditional literature, by McKeachie and by Weimer, illustrate the kinds of useful advice and admonitions you can put in practice to expand your understanding and use of FOPs.

In the points that follow, I suggest brief specifics about where to begin to blend your practices of FOPs with these traditional tips.

Extensions of Calming, Patience, and Timing

These simplest of FOPs are easiest to blend with traditional practices. Indeed, you may find that you have already been practicing some parts of what McKeachie and Weimer recommend in this regard. These are examples of parallels commonly seen by teachers in my programs:

- Beginning to prepare classroom materials early, well before feeling ready

- Making special efforts to involve students on the first days of class

- Pausing and stopping to notice student comprehension, to involve students in discussions and small-group activities

- Being patient

Extensions of Moderating Attachment, Reactivity, and Emotionality

These moderately complex FOPs also seem to be analogous:

- Dialoguing and exchanging observations among teachers

- Letting students do some of the work (e.g., introducing each other)

- Conducting early, informal evaluations to practice adaptive ways of eliciting useful, tolerable criticism

- Joining the conversation about teaching

Extensions of Resilience

Even this most complex level of FOPs, according to my program participants, suggests these links to the notions of McKeachie and Weimer:

- Limiting wasted effort (e.g., by increasing teaching awareness of what works and what doesn't)

- Practicing patience and tolerance (e.g., by allowing yourself to try alternative strategies even when you do not feel you need to work at your teaching)

- Practicing broadly, variably, flexibly (i.e., by trying various routines and ideas of teaching improvement experts such as McKeachie and Weimer, even when what you already do seems to work)

In the end, what will you have as a result of carrying out this practice of reading more books about teaching improvement and drawing parallels between them? More teaching awareness (as Weimer terms it). More ways of handling teaching and, so, more freedom and spontaneity as a teacher. More confidence and optimism borne of constantly improving your teaching. And, not least, more resilience through the inevitable problems that teachers encounter.

Rule 9: Welcome Learning and Change

10

Build Resilience by Limiting Wasted Efforts (Rule 10)

This tenth and final FOP (first-order principle) is the broadest and most flexible. It concerns the most important quality of learning how to work in the long run—the resilience that enables us to persist as caring, reflective teachers through obstacles and setbacks. The rule involved (Rule 10) is simultaneously simple and complex: Limit wasted efforts.

Notions that efficiency can be the healthiest and most productive way of working in the long run are anything but new. A pioneering economist came to much the same conclusion in his *Wealth of Nations* centuries ago:

> *The [person] who works so moderately as to be able to work constantly, not only preserves his [her] health the longest, but in the course of the year, executes the greatest quantity of work.*
> Adam Smith

More recently, a mere century ago, psychologists studied efficiency in a variety of activities ranging from athletics to creative efforts and established the facts: Resilient, productive work comes with pacing and rhythms that minimize fatigue while maximizing careful, economical practice. Contemporary research on expertise makes a similar point: Experts work and practice in brief regular sessions that limit fatigue and encourage opportunities to learn from mentors and other sources of coaching. Experts develop their greatness while learning from their mistakes; a striking commonality of masters in creative fields such as writing is that they produce lots of good work and almost as much mediocre stuff. This means that they learn by taking risks and that they practice resilience by persisting through each disappointment to the next exciting venture.

Something else is crucial to understanding efficiency. The healthiest, most creative, most productive work comes with moderation—not, as tradition would have us believe, with pressures for high rates of work and ever more output. Efficiency practiced efficiently requires patience and tolerance, not greed and intensity.

Efficient Practice in Higher Education
Most graduate students and professors work at their scholarly writing in demonstrably inefficient ways. They put off projects until pressured to rush and binge. They work themselves into frenzies of superficial reflection and depressing fatigue. You know the picture.

What keeps most of us from practicing more efficiency as teachers and writers? Teaching ourselves and our students how to *work* is not part of our culture; we expect people with true brilliance to come already equipped with the right stuff. And so we expect ourselves to know how to teach or write with only a minimum of experience and guidance—if we are to display the sort of genius requisite amongst the most admired of our colleagues. In fact, though, the most productive and happy of teachers and writers can be seen, on close examination, to exhibit the sorts of FOPs emphasized in this book while working, including economies of effort and resilience. Fortunately, these skills are quite transferrable to colleagues who otherwise make slower, more troublesome starts.

Recent research supports the value of FOPs. The great majority of exemplary teachers (those who work with the greatest self-reported ease and who elicit the most student approval and learning) have learned to rely on FOPs. They don't try to do too much. They know how to achieve simplicity combined with creativity. And they build strong, sensitive senses of audience. One other fact about excellent teachers is particularly relevant. As a rule, the small group of professors who teach with high ratings also fall into the category of the most productive writers/publishers. Excellence in one domain generalizes to the other (just as notions of FOP would predict). Similarly, those of us who tend to teach with the least approval also tend to publish the least. The great bulk of professors apparently falls between these two extremes, excelling in neither domain.

THE ROLE OF RESILIENCE

What has all this to do with resilience? Resilience depends, finally, on mastery of most all the FOPs we have already been considering. FOPs foster efficiency and lessen wasted efforts. Resilience, again, is as much a matter of not wasting efforts as of finding successes. My own studies of exemplary teachers and writers (i.e., individuals who excel at both by a variety of definitions) suggest how these mechanisms work. Efficient teachers waste little time with negative thinking, with overpreparing, or with procrastination that would have them doing nonessential things. (But they are not, incidentally, rigid or nonplayful.) They practice ways of finding successes (some as simple, initially, as lessening fatigue and heightening student civility). As a result, these teachers report that they grow more confident, more self-efficacious (i.e., better able to rebound from disappointments, more aware of how to get back on track quickly). Exemplars do something else we might want to mimic: They are close observers of other exemplars, and they study the ways that other people find success or failure.

Another way of appreciating the essences of resilience is looking once more to academic writers who succeed. Resilient writers (who evidence the most constancy, productivity, and health) work efficiently in the following ways:

- They devote only moderate amounts of time to writing but they do it regularly.

- They do it in brief sessions that require little warm-up time or foundering, and they stop in time to permit other daily activities such as socializing and exercising.

- They prewrite and plan and approximate writing enough so that prose writing goes quickly and painlessly.

- They work in comfort and mild happiness that exclude most of fatigue from working.

- They arrange conditions for working that encourage attentiveness to the task at hand (yet, they treat inevitable interruptions as occasions to take breaks and gain distance on what they were doing).

- They welcome most criticism, learn from it, and avoid overreacting to it.

- They let other people, even critics, do some of the work of writing.

- They work patiently towards excellence, but they tolerate failures and mediocrities along the way.

What they learn, more than anything else, is economy of action. This, again, is not news; the facts were well known before this century. Inefficiency is a matter of not knowing how to work.

> *[Jules] Amar....found that the accomplished journeyman normally adopted an efficient economy of motion that starkly contrasted with those of an apprentice, whose "chief defects are irregular and spasmodic action leading to unduly rapid fatigue."*
>
> Anson Rabinbach

Related facts: All these practices of FOPs make recovery from bad moods or traumatic events easier. In other words, all of them contribute to resilience. All encourage a greater emphasis on process orientation than product modes while working. Why does it matter? A process orientation helps turn the focus away from the outcome and redirects it toward acts/FOPs that lead to the product. A process orientation encourages learning from mistakes; it helps minimize wasted efforts.

The same tendencies pay rich dividends for teachers. They should. The same FOPs underlie all manner of efficient work. The same general principles build resilience. Try glancing back at the points just made about resilience in writing and look for parallels to work at teaching; it is time you did more of the work (just as you, when doing the teaching, can accomplish more for yourself and your students by getting them to do some of the work).

Consider this as a starting place: Both writing and teaching clearly fare better with a process orientation (as opposed to an outcomes stance). Working mostly in the moment and following careful but flexible plans provides many, many benefits: Lessened pressures to rush, increased awareness of your own ways of working, and better anticipation of how your audience will react. Less fatigue and more creativity and discovery. And so on. You already know these things.

What changes in Rule 10 is the emphasis on seeing the efficiencies interactively and on studying them more systematically. It isn't so demanding and complex as it sounds.

Practices for Rule 10
(Build Resilience by Limiting Wasted Efforts)

The essential part of this tenth stage is actually noticing efficient and wasteful actions in teaching. Much like the negative thoughts and the emotions of teaching we examined earlier, inefficiencies may seem invisible at first.

First, Monitor for Inefficiencies

Make a brief, daily habit (perhaps at the ends of work sessions) of noting inefficiencies. Common examples of things that teachers note in their journals include:

- Allowing too much distraction (e.g., an interloper to your office stays and chats beyond the brief message she/he intended to deliver)

- Overreacting to distractions (e.g., quitting a preparation session after having to stop for the noise of a lawn mower outside your window; thinking during most of the session about an argument you had earlier in the day)

- Working to fatigue (because you failed to pause, calm, slow down, and readjust your seating posture)

- Shifting too soon to product orientations including premature editing and anxieties about possibilities of criticism

- Working beyond preset stopping points and taking up the time that could have been used for other important things like socializing and exercising

- Putting off reasonable times for beginning conceptual outlines or other classroom materials by looking for still more references or motivation

- Working euphorically, hurriedly, and moving completely away from conceptual outlines and other plans

- Trying to prepare or grade in the evening, when you are tired, and when work will take needed time away from sleep

- Working obsessively, pessimistically

- Forgetting that you, ultimately, decide what is stressfully debilitating and what is not by how you choose to interpret events

  It isn't so much what happens to you that matters. It's how you react to it.

                                                    Pat Riley

Resilient teachers and writers learn from mistakes and disappointments in several ways. In one, they examine things like criticisms and rejections closely, calmly. By listening reflectively to useful information and requesting more constructive suggestions for change, they act economically: They change in adaptive directions. They don't invest energy and time in overreacting, defensively, to the criticism or failure. Resiliency isn't just a God-given trait of inner strength; it is more the product of learning what matters in the moment. It even includes the remarkable tolerance of attending to how other academics find success.

Resilient teachers and writers practice brief daily sessions. These build strong habits and the stronger the habit (and pleasure), the greater the likelihood that it will persist through distractions, traumas, and sicknesses. Or (as the most meaningful measure of resilience), that teachers and writers will rebound quickly to regular habits and attitudes.

The final economy in resilience is most obviously an economy. Writers with the most constancy and happiness generally work in brief sessions that minimize fatigue and inefficient practices. Brief daily sessions are easier to resume than are binges.

I could continue but you get the point. Besides, these are things best discovered for yourself.

Second, Make a Social Contract for
Discovering and Appreciating Wasted Efforts

Brief, regular discussions about wasted efforts make the process even more economical. They impel you to do the noticing of your own inefficiencies so that you will have something to report at the next meeting. The reports of others will help alert you to wasted efforts you had overlooked in your own teaching.

Third, Put Increasing Emphasis on Efficiencies

There are limitations in looking too closely or too long at inefficiencies. They demoralize (especially if they seem to dominate your actions). They confuse (sometimes it is hard to distinguish between an inefficiency and leisure). And they don't always tell us what to do in their place. So in the long run, efficient teachers tend to emphasize what they do well and try to add more and more economies.

- Habits of preteaching that bring motivation and imagination

- Pauses, stretches, and refocuses that refresh

- Brief daily sessions that become habitual and enjoyable (e.g., "I actually look forward to them")

- Spontaneity and interactiveness in teaching that bring excitement, discovery, and self-esteem

- Conceptual outlines that make teaching quick and easy

- Process orientations that encourage mild happiness and a near absence of negative thinking

- Resilience in the wake of disruptions and disappointments

- Immersion in revisions as a delightful experience of exercising your listening skills and perfectionistic tendencies at the right time

Fourth, Build Self-Esteem and Resilience in Other Domains that Affect Teaching

In the longer run, efficient teachers notice that their work cannot occur in isolation from the rest of their lives. Two things prove to be especially crucial and worth monitoring. One is sleep; chronic insomnia and tiredness undermine efficient teaching. The other is physical conditioning. Teachers who exercise regularly are more resilient in the face of stresses, including the traumas that commonly derail and dismay. Teachers who maintain self-disciplines such as regular exercise (e.g., weight training, meditation and Yoga, aerobic training) show higher self-esteem, self-efficacy (i.e., beliefs that they can succeed and practice at finding ways to work efficiently, resiliently), and patience/tolerance.

In my programs for new TAs and novice faculty, this last suggestion elicits an understandable objection. The point is often made as this teacher said it: "I just want to be a reasonably good teacher. You want to remodel my whole life." Sometimes the reservation gets made this way: "Isn't there escape from rules and hard work anywhere in all this? Isn't there room for magic here somewhere? My answer to both questions is a tranquil "yes."

Efficiencies in working do tend to generalize to other aspects of working and living. My own studies of junior professors learning FOPs show that they readily apply the same basic rules to both teaching and writing. Moreover, they perform better in each sphere than if they had worked on only one. The same generality holds true for practice at sleeping more efficiently, restfully, painlessly. It holds for becoming habitual exercisers, and for working at mundane things like house cleaning and painting interior walls. And so on. What matters most in these extensions of efficiencies is that they do not take away control, or turn teachers into efficiency zealots who automatize every aspect of their lives.

But they do allow more free time for fun and for not doing. This is where the authentic magic comes—from the discipline that makes some of the work easier and briefer, from the happiness and playfulness in working that merge easily with leisure and sudden discoveries. Once teachers practice these efficiencies more generally, they realize something else: Nothing will change lives more profoundly than becoming a "real teacher." A regular habit of learning from coaches and critics, of discovering worthwhile things to say, brings astonishing results.

Certain outcomes are most commonly reported and valued after a few years of practice at efficiencies: 1) self-education in terms of seeing connections and themes at higher levels, in simpler and more usable ways; 2) self-esteem and self-efficacy; 3) more output from less time spent working at teaching and writing; 4) good teaching and writing; and 5) painless teaching and writing.

Then consider things as they usually are without such practices: Even those of us expected to do little more than teaching are not assured of teaching well; in usual practice, no one will coach or model for us in the kinds of meaningful ways that writers learn from editors and reviewers and colleagues. Moreover, those of us most likely to do little more than teach are unlikely to learn the sorts of FOPs that could generalize to other skills. Those of us who focus on teaching to the exclusion of other things work most inefficiently, busily, stressfully.

But what of existing programs to facilitate teaching such as instructional development programs? They remain little-known. Most of them are amiable and nonthreatening; few can cite evidence for their effectiveness in improving teaching skills. Fewer still can claim to help newcomers on the margins to work more effectively as both teachers and as writers.

There is an encouraging point in these discouraging revelations. Teachers who work efficiently enough to write effectively *can* enhance their self-esteem and status in both spheres. And even teachers who choose not to write can find far more satisfaction and growth with FOPs based on writing. To thrive as teachers, then, we may need to look beyond teaching to other activities. None is probably better than writing. Why? It teaches discovery, clear thinking, and effective communication. It demands good work habits in the midst of competing demands. It rewards. (The next chapter provides more details.)

Fifth, Work Playfully

> *The most creative people are the ones with the least separation in daily life between work and play.*
>
> Eric Erickson

In other words, link your thoughts and actions as a teacher to other things you do. Try, for example, mentioning more of your scholarly/research interests as they relate to what you say in class. (It turns out that students especially value and reward this sort of connecting—the links provide a better sense of who you are and they help clarify concepts with examples.) And anticipate the reasons you might resist this bit of broadening and loosening your teaching: First, you may suppose you are too far behind, too busy to add personal accounts (but you already know the rebuttal to that bit of irrationality). Second, you might worry that mentions of what interests you most is an act of selfishness (realize, though, that teachers least likely to bring themselves and their interests into class are most likely to suffer poor evaluations of their teaching). Good teaching *is*, after all, a bit selfish. So is learning.

Sixth, Be Patient

> *To become reflective and mindful practitioners, we need to learn to let go of involvement in our thoughts and feelings while plunging ourselves, mind and body, into the center of teaching and learning. This is no easy task.*
>
> Robert Tremmel

Said another way, teaching requires risk-taking and, in the short-run, some discomforts and disappointments.

Seventh, Consider the Outcomes of Empirical Studies about Teaching Improvement

For example, try plodding through one of my experimental accounts of FOPs as interventions. It is one thing to talk about these things and another to measure how they actually work. I include a modest example in the next chapter. It, like so much of this book (and of good teaching), repeats basic principles in slightly different ways.

Rule 10: Build Resilience by Limiting Wasted Efforts

11

Research Showing that FOPs Work

What, beyond the routines of regular practice we have already seen, helps strengthen FOPs (first-order principles)? Practicing them more broadly, across different domains. Here, in Chapter 11, we look at a powerful strategy, of generalizing the FOPs we have learned as teachers (in Chapters 1-10) to practicing fundamentally similar ways of working as scholarly writers. Surprising as this move may seem, I have found that a maximally effective education for new teachers includes a corresponding program for learning how to work as writers. So far as I can tell, neither teaching nor writing occurs in a vacuum for newcomers to academe. Neglect of either one undermines performance in the other—at both the graduate and new faculty stages of careers.

In this last chapter, I show how teaching and writing interrelate. And how mastering both sets of related FOPs makes their individual performances more productive and enjoyable.

In what lies ahead, I present an abbreviated version of an unusual study of teaching improvement (Boice, 1995a); it is one of the few in the literature to show measurable, lasting effects of interventions. It is probably the only such study to focus on economies and simplicities of teaching. And it is surely the first demonstration of the mutual benefits in applying FOPs to both teaching and writing.

I present these procedures and data for two reasons: First, I want to show you evidence that reasonably simple programs can induce worthwhile improvements when novice professors need them most. (After all, a key emphasis of this book is that advice about teaching improvement should be based on research, not just conjecture.) Second, I hope to induce you to expand your understanding of the FOPs about teaching in ever-widening ways. Teachers in my programs have consistently told me that they didn't really "get it" until they applied similar FOPs to teaching and to writing. That move proved to be the start of even greater efficiencies including a realization that teaching and writing are much the same in terms of basic ways of working. What gets learned in one and applied to the other ends up working even better for the first case.

A RATIONALE FOR THE STUDY

Consider why most newcomers to the professoriate neither receive nor want much help as teachers (even if you never fit this category). They typically put off instructional development while they wait for success as writers (Boice, 1992b).

But there are hidden perils in postponing teaching improvements for long: Early failures in the classroom hinder potentials for lasting teaching careers (McKeachie, 1994). And the supposed benefit of putting off teaching improvement—getting more writing done— rarely repays the sacrifice. Why? So long as busy, tiring days persist, procrastination dominates; most new faculty manage little writing during their first few years on campus. Without the self-efficacy borne of reasonable mastery in both teaching and writing, new faculty remain doubtful and inefficient, rushing but never quite catching up, rarely meeting their career plans or potentials. Promise shown at hiring can soon deteriorate into a pattern of uninvolvement that persists through midcareer, where neither teaching nor writing are matters of pride (Boice, 1993b).

If you will, join me in a few assumptions: Deep, enduring improvement in neither teaching nor writing occurs in isolation; success at both teaching and writing can depend on similar kinds of collegial supports and on self-management; both need good starts; both might build on similar FOPs; and, each could augment the other. Pace (1987), an expert on academics, puts it simply: Good things go together.

I tested those notions by helping junior faculty manage writing fluency and then, soon after, by transferring the FOPs involved to teaching. Why use this ordering? For one thing, new faculty more readily opt for help with writing than with teaching because of entrenched reward and status patterns. Another reason for starting with writing is that writing theorists offer the kinds of good models and researched principles usually undersupplied to teachers (Ronkowski, 1993). The third reason is most compelling. Graduate students and new faculty rarely feel they have time for both programs at once. No matter that they *do* have time or that they needlessly dichotomize teaching and writing. What does matter is finding ways to involve novices in both kinds of programs quickly, while their experiences are still formative. The fourth, final, reason is the most practical. Newcomers who learn to work efficiently at writing find more time to use similar strategies as teachers. Writing can be the hook that pulls otherwise reluctant teachers into instructional development programs.

The initial steps in my own attempts to promote this interconnection between teaching and writing began with questions and preliminary researches.

INQUIRIES AND INSIGHTS

Two decades of research and practice shaped the "writing-then-teaching" paradigm I describe here. (At the same time, as we will see, I developed "teaching-then-writing" programs for the sake of comparison.) I began by asking if faculty development should include help with scholarly writing (in part because no one else had in systematic, assessed ways).

Do Many New Faculty Need Help with Scholarly Writing?

A misimpression created by the debate on teaching versus research perpetuates the need for this question. Tradition supposes that new faculty (cf., curiously, new graduate students) arrive on campus well-trained as writers/publishers but not as teachers; presumably, only teaching is left behind at the starting gate. In fact, novice professors start out woefully underprepared in either survival skill (Boice, 1992b). Most academicians publish little, if at all, over the course of their careers (Braxton and Bayer, 1986); this failure to meet original plans for scholarly writing can exact an enormous price. When junior faculty do not receive praise as researchers/writers, they are unlikely to find it elsewhere on campus (Boice, 1993b). When new graduate students struggle at both teaching and writing, they risk long delays in finishing dissertations and lessened professional opportunities (Boyle, 1996).

That traditional belief, about overtraining in graduate school as researcher/scholars, holds so tenaciously that I found myself having to defend the faculty development programs I had devised for writers. But repeated inquiries produced an abundance of data to support those programs. In sum, the majority of new faculty, especially women and minorities, report experiences of surprising neglect as apprentice researchers/writers (from both graduate advisors and committees). Dissertations are normally completed, if at all, amid great uncertainty and procrastination. Then, as newcomers to their first positions in the professoriate, most novices (whether with doctorates from prestigious research universities or not) privately express reservations about what kinds of scholarship to do (the modal type of comment: "how do I know if I'm asking the right questions?"), about how to work efficiently ("is it possible to get any writing done unless I get a year off to do nothing else?"), or how to format it for publication ("I'm not entirely sure I know what a publishable manuscript is supposed to look like").

The results of this undertraining and undersupporting in research/writing appear dramatically. Over 80% of new hires at the research and comprehensive campuses I have studied fail to manage even minimally acceptable outputs of scholarly writing (i.e., the equivalent of one 20-40 page manuscript per annum) during their first several years on the job (and often, beyond). Other results of that neglect emerge in more subtle ways. Much as new teachers work with what Weimer (1991) calls a lack of teaching awareness, new scholars work with a lack of writing awareness. They do not know how to write without bingeing and suffering. They cannot manage writing (or teaching), at least in the short run, without bingeing and, so, sacrificing social life, health, and leisure. They do not know, except in vague hopes for the benefits of experience, how to change. They develop little resilience as writers or as teachers.

Related outcomes are predictable: Most novices make writing their highest priority but do little or none for years. Newcomers delay writing until ideal conditions can be found (e.g., large blocks of uninterrupted time during summer vacations) but then use those interludes to recuperate. Most novices, when they try to write at all, rush it and dislike it; when they submit their writing to editors, they grow discouraged with the seeming cruelty and capriciousness of reviewers. And most imagine they must master writing on their own, in private. The same pattern holds for teaching, less visibly.

How Do Some New Faculty Succeed as Writers on Their Own?

I asked this question to get clues about how the usual pattern of new faculty starts could be improved. Novices who displayed quick success as writers *and* as teachers, some 10-13% of newcomers in my study cohorts, did provide indicators about what their less successful peers needed to do (Boice, 1991). Overall, exemplars showed four uniquely adaptive and resilient tendencies as writers; we already know them, more-or-less, from our exposure to FOPs of teaching.

1. These newcomers worked more deliberately at moderation (e.g., they put less pressure on themselves for perfection or fast results).

2. They planfully managed balance in their work (e.g., they spent as much time at planning and rehearsing writing as at writing).

3. They worked with constancy (i.e., they wrote regularly).

4. When they followed rules or programs, they made room for feelings of spontaneity and enjoyment.

Exemplars, unlike normal new faculty, did not experience first years on campus as overloading them with work, as isolating them from colleagues and ideas, as derailing them from their intended careers or personal lives.

What Factors Best Help Writers Find Fluency and Satisfaction?

Even with information about what intelligent novices (as cognitive researchers call them) do, I saw only part of the solution for many years. I started my writing programs, much as others had, by emphasizing ways of forcing. When rewards or punishments were strong enough, even the most reluctant writers worked regularly and productively—but not always after the formal program had ceased (Boice, 1992a). Health researchers have been learning the same lesson: merely kick-starting a new habit is not enough for lasting results; techniques for initiation must be integrated with methods of maintenance (McCaul, Glasgow, & O'Neill, 1992). In the end, the sort of resilience that keeps us performing adaptive new habits is most important.

After many more years of testing to see what worked best to keep writers writing, I noticed some other things: First, lasting progress comes gradually, not in a few lengthy workshops, but in regular practice. Second, effective help with writing starts well before actual writing begins (e.g., in finding motivation and ideas). Third, effective help also extends well after usual programs for writers end (e.g., ways of coping with criticism). Fourth, the most basic skills of writing are more a matter of how to work than how to write.

FUNDAMENTAL STRATEGIES FOR EFFICIENT, COMFORTABLE WRITING

First, a caution. I do not see this scheme as the only way to help writers; it is, though, unique for its extensive development and empirical testing. Then, another proviso. Because of space limitations, I report here the progress of only 16 academic writers. (They were drawn from a larger sample of 52 participants selected for extensive analysis—Boice, 1994). These 16 are representative of junior faculty for their academic disciplines and genders.

A final caution. While every participant was treated individually for special needs, I here present only the basic interventions that sufficed to bring substantial development for all but a handful of new faculty who persisted. These FOPs are the "writerly rules" that transfer readily to teaching (Boice, 1995b).

The fine details of my methods and of participants' phenomenological experiences appear elsewhere (Boice, 1994; 1995a). In brief: I assemble a few small groups of four to eight volunteers each year, often somewhat homogeneous in demographics. Everyone enters the program promising to stay the course, to attend almost all weekly group meetings (even during busy times like midterm exams), to form partnerships with at least one other group member for interim calls of support and encouragement, and to arrange brief, daily times for working. Not everyone manages this entire discipline; about a third of starters typically quit before the end of the formal program for a variety of reasons that boil down to busyness and doubt. Nonetheless, this is a tolerable retention rate for so demanding a developmental program, one where I personally recruit new faculty who would otherwise not volunteer (and who are, generally, the neediest).

During my repeated assessments of how writers progress (e.g., Boice, 1992a), I winnowed techniques into six reliable stages of treatment. (Each stage can take as long as two months; some groups meet more frequently to compress the entire course into a few months.) In what follows I present a brief explanation about the purpose of each stage, a memorable rule for the most essential acts, and the specific outcomes measured. (Note that in this particular study I condensed the ten stages of this book into six. Either way seems to work as well.)

As you journey through this first part of the study, on writing, please keep something in mind: I could just as well be talking about teaching…as I soon will. That is, what you will learn about writing applies to teaching (and, provides fresh reminders of what we have already learned about teaching in earlier chapters). What lies ahead in this last chapter is about building the special kind of resilience that comes from generalizing FOPs across domains to teaching. Patience, patience, patience.

FIRST STAGE: FINDING MOTIVATION
(RULE: PREPARE IN PATIENT, TIMELY FASHION—BEFOREHAND)

Motivation comes first in the program because: a) It, more immediately than anything else, distinguishes quick starters as writers. Exemplars rarely struggle for impetus or momentum; b) The lack of good habits for conjuring motivation and the usual myths about it keeps more writers from writing fluently than any other factor. Writers who wait for Muses and feelings of enthusiasm, who delay and then force themselves to work under deadlines, who make their acts of getting ready for writing unreinforcing, undermine their motivation and their writing; c) Exemplars suffer least from impatience, the nemesis of reliable motivation.

We begin group discussions by talking about some remarkable aspects of exemplars: They, like other motivated writers, prepare and work patiently, with the openness and flexibility of mild happiness that facilitates problem solving (Oatley & Jenkins, 1992). They initiate projects early, before feeling fully confident or clear; they expect durable motivation to develop after they are already working. And, exemplars do other things highly predictive of reliable motivation: They typically write in brief sessions that help keep ideas fresh in mind, day-to-day, and that tire them less than marathon bouts. They even find ways to make preparations and work rewarding (e.g., starting by writing easily published manuscripts like annotated bibliographies that give writers the confidence of knowing their stuff).

Mastering this sort of enjoyable regularity in writing demands an overlooked skill, just as in teaching: Stopping. Exemplars are quickest to appreciate the value of timely stopping—at the ends of regularly scheduled sessions, and en route (to pause and relax). They even notice the value of stopping their day's writing, in the middle of sentences and paragraphs. Why? With the task incomplete, they think about it in the interim; when they next work, writers face an easy restart compared to the outlined start of a new sentence or paragraph. All these variations of timely stopping help build motivation by keeping writers unfatigued and ready to resume the next session.

Writers practice and chart two specific acts in stage one:

1. Starting means preparing and beginning on schedule, regardless of feeling ready. Participants schedule and practice brief, daily sessions (often no more than 15 minutes per day at first; rarely more than 60-120 minutes in the long run). When they cannot write, they approximate (e.g., free-form journal entries, conceptually outlining ideas for writing projects, or annotating relevant writing).

2. Stopping has two related subparts, one about pausing and one about halting on schedule, even when not feeling ready. Stopping means practicing planned pauses while working, (such as to stretch and breathe meditatively). Stopping also means halting at or just before the preset end time, usually before finishing a sentence, better yet before completing a paragraph.

Measures of Motivation

There are two objective measures of stage one (Building motivation), both of them about constancy: 1) An index of how regularly writers worked at writing-related tasks on a daily schedule and stopped in timely fashion; and 2) An output index of writing-related materials (measured in terms of verified, typed-page-equivalents). And there are two subjective measures of self-perceived comfort for writers, each indexed with self-rating scales (1–10 scoring): 1) Estimates of patience while readying to write; and, 2) Ratings of the excitement and intensity managed for writing that day.

In these measures there is, then, a layer within a layer of what remains an essentially simple scheme for assessing progress. Constancy is measured objectively (as brief, daily sessions carried out on schedule; as outputs per writing day). Comfort is measured subjectively (as self-ratings of patience/readiness; and as self-ratings of excitement/intensity). Those second measures, for both constancy and comfort, represent a dimension that writers initially insist is essential to their success and satisfaction. They see quantity of output and excitement as more important than reliability and patience.

We compromise between differing interests by including both theirs and mine. I, on the one hand, want them to emphasize constancy as the habit of writing regularly. I want them to find comfort by way of mild emotions and restful rhythms. I prefer that they put off productivity measures until sound work habits are in place. They, on the other hand, want constancy defined to focus on large outputs ("I have lots of writing to catch up on"). And they want meanings of comfort broadened to include the inspired, exhilarating experience they imagine must motivate good writing. I label the former category as measures of moderation and the latter as measures of maximization.

SECOND STAGE: FINDING IMAGINATION
(RULE: PRACTICE REINFORCING ACTS OF DISCOVERY)

Imagination begins with finding good problems to solve (Perkins, 1985), and it brings rewarding novelty and cleverness to work. Many new faculty feel deficiently imaginative in ways that inhibit their spontaneity and subvert their self-assurance (Boice, 1993a). Imagination enhances and maintains motivation; without the reinforcement provided by interesting ideas and connections, motivation fades. Imagination provides the enthusiasm of having something to say and the comfort or excitement of knowing it may be worth saying. Imagination's constancy comes from the patience of waiting while reexamining what can be said, of putting off closure while arranging even more creativity. Because imagination distributes much of the hard work of writing to preliminaries, it can make writing easier, better organized, and more comfortable (Flower & Hayes, 1981). How does maximizing fit here? Maximizers argue that imagination fares best with high levels of emotion and their "hot cognitions" or excited, impelling thoughts (Brand, 1989).

Most methods for building imagination favor moderation. The best-known of these come from composition researchers and social scientists (Flower, 1990; Mills, 1959; Murray, 1978). Their essential notions are prescribed as patient preliminaries to prose writing: 1) Brief, daily sessions of conceptual outlining and organizing ideas for a writing project; 2) Daily sessions of prewriting (i.e., putting ideas into conceptual outlines with approximations of prose); and 3) Regular practice at revising plans and outlines before (and after) moving to prose. Researchers on writing offer a telling fact about the value of these patient preliminaries: Expertise comes with a goal-directedness and with a working-through to solutions *before* committing to prose; in contrast, mediocrity (and its unimaginativeness) comes with impatient demands to get rid of constraints and plans in writing (Scardamalia and Bereiter, 1985). In my own work with new faculty, I hear the same, impatient push for spontaneity and immediacy—as in this modal comment of writers who continue to get little done: "I want my writing to be fast, and easy, and brilliant."

Measures of Imagination

There are two objective measures for stage two (Imagination): 1) The first charts habitualness (percentages) at carrying out writing-related preliminaries during two weeks or more of brief daily sessions. In initial sessions, writers collect, file, and reorganize ideas into various problem formulations while preparing for a new or revived writing project. They next contract for ten or more brief daily sessions of prewriting (i.e., amassing approximations of what will become prose); this prewriting usually consists of free writing and conceptual outlining. Then, they schedule 5–10 writing sessions for revisions of both plans and prewriting. 2) The second measure charts outputs of writing-related materials (in typed-page equivalents). The self-ratings of comfort and satisfaction for stage two resemble those of stage one: 1) Daily estimates of success at managing patience in preparations, particularly in terms of delaying closure about what will be written (1–10 scale), and 2) Daily estimates of how much excitement and brilliance are generated (against maximal amounts) for this preliminary work.

In stage two, I coach writers in at least three ways. First, I remind them of what exemplars and other successful writers do in terms of imagination (i.e., they constantly practice noticing and noting things during other activities that can be related to ideas for writing). Second,

I caution them against the impatience and pressure of expecting rapid, perfect results. Third, I encourage their quests for excitement, but always with a caution: "Try things like bingeing and hot cognitions whole-heartedly, but occasionally give the alternative of moderation an honest trial."

THIRD STAGE: FINDING FLUENCY
(RULE: PRACTICE WRITING REGULARLY, PLANFULLY)

Fluency is best appreciated by new faculty in terms of its opposite, dysfluency. Novice writers hope for fluent outpourings but too often experience inhibitions, hesitancies, inefficiencies, blocks. Teachers long for something similar—reliably effortless flows of enthusiasm, ideas, and clarity. Research shows that fluency suffers most from a lack of constancy in work (Boice, 1993c). So does that relative of fluency, resiliency.

Another thing that perpetuates dysfluencies is lack of knowledge. We rarely teach the skills of efficiency and productivity to newcomers (Bullough, Knowles, & Crow, 1991), perhaps because we see fluency as mysterious or inborn. Maladaptive habits also sustain dysfluencies. Usual attempts to induce fluency by rushing make it seem all the more uncontrollable; writing is put off because busyness, real or imaginary, displaces timely work (Boice, 1989; 1992a). New faculty often put it like this: "I'm so busy, I'm going crazy. I'm too busy to write while I'm teaching and meeting my family obligations. Are you kidding me?"

The following exercises help build fluency: 1) Practice brief, daily sessions that combine prewriting, prose writing, and rewriting. 2) Deliberately practice occasional binges (i.e., more than five hours of continuously intense work) when big blocks of undisrupted time become available. 3) Practice setting clear goals for productivity within sessions (commonly a one page-equivalent of notes, outlines, revisions, or writing; under maximization, twice as much). 4) Plan short-term use, for up to two months continuously, of contingency management to instill a regular habit of writing. Contingency management works by making something that is already probable and enjoyable contingent on first doing scheduled writing for the day. Because they force work and eventually associate aversiveness with writing, contingencies operate best in moderation (and in the short run).

Measures of Fluency

Objective measures of fluency for stage three (Finding fluency): 1) Percentages of brief daily sessions carried out on schedule; and 2) Percentages of brief daily sessions where maximized goals for productivity were met (usually based on an aim of 2.0 pages per hour; cf. a moderate goal of 1.0 pages per brief daily sessions). Self-rating measures: 1) Self-estimates of fluency (1–10 scale) defined as ease, readiness, flow, and clarity of writing (and contrasted with prior experiences of blocking at writing). 2) Ratings of excitement and effort expended, as judged (1–10) against maximal possible enjoyment and intensity (for both brief sessions and binges). None of these measures (of habituality, of outputs, of ease, or of intensity) is completely new, but here they are emphasized.

FOURTH STAGE: FINDING CONTROL
(RULE: WORK WITH MILD HAPPINESS AND
SUPPORTIVE SURROUNDS)

Participants in the program rehearse strategies for self-control that derive from what exemplars do. In one set of exercises, writers learn to limit their "self-handicapping" scripts (e.g., discounting their own abilities to write while maintaining unrealistically high standards of success—Baumeister & Scher, 1988). In a second set, they moderate self-defeating acts by supplanting irrational thinking with rational solutions such as constructing more realistic, optimistic expectations as writers. This strategy is called Rational-Emotive Therapy (RET) and is a widely successful form of self-help that requires no training or therapist (Ellis & Knaus, 1977). In a third set of exercises, writers practice monitoring and modifying their moods. Sometimes they deliberately conjure the excited rushing of hypomania (a near-state of mania). In other writing sessions, writers aim for mild happiness (i.e., they moderate the euphoria that otherwise turns to fatigue and dysphoria—Jamison, 1993).

Participants also practice externally-oriented methods of control. In one, they arrange more pleasant, comfortable, and helpful surrounds for writing sessions (but not until writing goals are met for the day). They add, say, personal decorations, comfortable seating, and temporarily closed office doors. In another exercise, writers keep interruptions such as phone calls brief (but without insisting on their complete absence; efficient writers welcome mild distractions as a relief from narrowness and rushing). And, in a third set of sessions, they work with social supports readily available (commonly, they schedule writing times with another writer present and working quietly).

In this fourth stage, on control, writers practice the following specific acts (all are matters of constancy and comfort): 1) They habitually monitor for (and correct) irrational thoughts and self-defeating acts at the outsets, midpoints, and ends of writing sessions by noting their inefficiency, disputing them in writing, and noting a more rational alternative to pursue (see Boice, 1994, for more details); 2) They pause to stretch and to notice symptoms both of fatigue (postural discomfort, eye strain, keyboard error rates) and of anxiety (fear, tension, impatience); 3) They moderate their attachment to the content of writing by looking for signs, first, of unreasonable impatience with progress, second, of overreaction to minor distractions and criticisms, and, third, of overly quick and intense satisfaction with the writing (something expert writers are unlikely to show—Brand, 1989); and, 4) They end, not begin, daily sessions by arranging their work sites to improve their esthetics and usefulness for subsequent sessions (e.g., stick-on notes about what to do next).

Measures of Control

In stage four (Finding control), the objective measures include: 1) Percentages of scheduled times in and around brief daily sessions actually used to monitor and correct irrationalities (using checklists that remind writers of the occasions for such acts); 2) Percentages of sessions with high outputs that meet maximized goal levels. Self-ratings indexed perceived concomitants of comfort and satisfaction for the objective measures just outlined: 1) Percentages of sessions dominated by mild happiness/optimism; 2) Percentages of sessions ruled by strong intensity and euphoria.

Success at control brings an unexpected result: Less isolation in work at writing. By moving away from intense self-focus to noticing the effects of moods, habits, and surrounds on their writing, writers become more outgoing and more sensitive to audience.

Fifth Stage: Finding Audience
(Rule: Listen to understand, then to be understood)

Audience (appreciating what readers expect and need; finding support and acceptance from readers) is difficult because most writers try to work in complete privacy. The usually unwritten rule for genius explains why: To be credited as brilliant, writing must be done with little obvious effort or assistance (Skinner, 1971). But seclusion is not merely inefficient and likely to misdirect. Its resulting shyness carries the risk of overreaction to criticism or praise (Beck, Rush, Shaw, & Emery, 1979). With that irritability, in turn, comes suspiciousness, more distancing from audiences, and a reluctance to have one's work evaluated (Kuiper, Olinger, & Martin, 1988). What begins as the seclusion that seems necessary for clear thinking can grow into blocking (Boice, 1993c).

Exemplars model efficient ways of finding audience. They, far more readily than other newcomers, avoid isolation, misdirection, and surprise by asking more questions about audiences ("What have you learned about how to anticipate the reactions of reviewers for this journal?"). They show why acts of efficiency need not be impersonal and socially unskilled (e.g., exemplars pause to listen carefully, reflectively during encounters with colleagues and students). They more often ask for help in finding the best problems ("What do you think I should emphasize in all this?"). They solicit early, informal evaluations of their plans and writing ("Does this seem to be on the right track?"). As they try these things, they chance upon a hidden key to audience: Exemplars let colleagues (and students) do some of the work, and even collaborate with them. (But here too, moderation is crucial; new faculty, especially women and minorities, must clearly do some writing on their own.)

The basic exercises for stage five (Audience) are simple but difficult; they require more practice than most new faculty initially suppose: 1) Scheduled sharings of early plans and drafts during the plan/outline that includes approximations of prose); 2) Occasional collaborations where writing (say, of grant proposals) occurs in intense, rapid, sustained fashion—well beyond usual limits for brief daily sessions; 3) Brief, regular practice of strategies for coping with criticism (e.g., finding something in even the worst-case rejections with which to agree—see Boice, 1994); 4) Deliberate, periodic quests to find colleagues and students with whom to share and explain samples of writing.

Here I remind writers that the essential aim is achieving an efficient and pleasing balance between the private and public sides of writing. (The essence of that balance is the rule for this stage borrowed, above, from Covey, 1989). The difficult part of this move is toward what psychotherapists and composition researchers call externalization. This externalizing away from self-focus and seclusion, is facilitated by starting sooner at putting thoughts out in print, first for one's own understanding and then for other readers (Elbow, 1992). Externalizing also helps stabilize writers' moods by directing consciousness away from the self-focus that risks depression and anxiety (Ingram, 1990). It even wards off rejection as writers read aloud and talk about their formative writing to anticipate how audiences will respond. Why? When writers join public conversations, they discover what is usually said in a discipline, how it is best written by its admired writers, and what still needs saying (Olson, 1992).

Measures of Finding Audience

Objective measures for stage five (Audience) are: 1) Combined percentages of two kinds of scheduled exercises carried out as extensions of brief daily sessions—early sharings of materials and practice at learning from criticism of formative writing. 2) Percentages of exercises in finding audience accompanied by high levels of productivity (e.g., for pages written collaboratively). Self-ratings: 1) Percentages of brief daily sessions that meet preset goal levels for finding ease with three kinds of exercises in audience: in seeking early advice and support, in letting others do some of the work, in learning from criticism. 2) Percentages of brief sessions that meet preset goal levels of two kinds of high excitement: in sharing writing and in experiencing prospects for impressing audiences.

A warning is in order: Audience disinterest and disapproval, even if fleeting, elicit regressions to old habits and beliefs more surely than any other experience of writers (and teachers) in the program. This is a crucial turning point at which I coach writers to see disappointment as more informative than adversarial. This re-seeing is an essential act of efficiency and resilience. (And these are what the preceding chapter was about.)

SIXTH STAGE: FINDING RESILIENCE
(RULE: REINVENT YOURSELF VIA SELF-STUDY)

Resilience, as we know, means working through obstacles. It means learning from setbacks, instead of giving up prematurely. Exemplars are primed to excel at this sort of durability because of already familiar practices: They are less attached to content and less controlled by strong moods and fatigue, so they are less likely to overreact to distractions and criticisms. They are flexibly efficient, notably at doing several things simultaneously (Bluedorn, Kaufman, & Lane, 1992) and at sorting out what most needs doing. They are patient about completing projects and about publicly demonstrating expertise in them (and so, less hurried and perfectionistic).

Exemplars also plan ahead for occasions where they will be likely to relapse from new habits; they anticipate probable obstacles, and they rehearse ways to use setbacks as cues for recalibrating and for getting back on track. In particular, they make precommitments about how they will react, about how they will avoid impulsive returns to bad habits (Logue, 1994). To do this, they study themselves with a special eye to weeding out wasted efforts and poor choices in their writing. At this point, writers begin to see that resilience is undermined mostly by poor planning, poor work habits, and other inefficiencies.

To narrow the scope of resilience so that everyone practices the same essentials, I ask writers to do four things as parts of regular practice at writing:

1. To vary the pace of work to include both reflective calm and generative euphoria.

2. To make ongoing estimates of economy at writing (cf. time and effort spent on distractions, blind alleys, errors).

3. To work planfully at enjoyment while writing to incorporate pleasant experiences into work (Eisenberger, 1992).

4. To add a few moments to each afterwork session to note what needs to be kept in mind for the next time (Langer, 1989) and what was done well.

Why the emphasis on planfulness? Writers who continuously reassess their progress toward concrete goals work the most efficiently, flexibly, successfully. Those who work less mindfully by refusing to look ahead, calmly, run the peril of facing new challenges where they suddenly lose their direction and momentum (Scardamalia & Bereiter, 1985).

Measures of Resilience

Objective measures of finding resilience are percentage-based indices of constancy: 1) Instances against plans of entering post-session notes for deciding what needs revision, for spotting what deserves commendation; 2) Instances against maximal plans for writing quickly, productively. Self-ratings: 1) Assessments of self-efficacy (with two rating anchors—most time was spent economically/confidently vs. most time was spent inefficiently/unconfidently); 2) Judgments of generating strong excitement and momentum that could carry a writer past hurdles.

This sixth and final stage (Resilience) is a special occasion for group members to examine the accumulated trends shown in the data, their own and those collected from other groups.

ESSENTIAL OUTCOMES OF THE WRITING PROGRAM
In terms of these basics, participants managed more than enough output and success as writers to meet departmental expectations for retention and tenure. All but a few learned to enjoy writing so much that they usually looked forward to brief daily sessions.

Writers at this reflective juncture generally wanted to look again at a schematic of the stages, of the writerly rules, and of the definitions of measures. With this paradigm in view, writers spontaneously made connections (the modal first-remark is quoted here): "I'm beginning to notice that this says how much we do is not as important as how we do it. Right?" In other words, writers had learned how to work.

Participants saw other surprisingly broad implications, especially about applying ways of working to other domains: "These rules are so elementary, so essential. I can sort of imagine how each one is going to work for teaching."

Other insights came from summaries of results over the project. Table 1 shows the overall trends of progress averaged across all 16 writers. To provide indices that tracked progress across stages, I had writers record four global measures over the whole program: 1) Habitualness of carrying out brief, daily sessions (bds); 2) Productivity of brief, daily sessions; 3) Self-ratings of combined relaxation and exteriorization; and, 4) Self-ratings of combined excitement and hard work. These global results indicate solid success in helping junior faculty write reliably, productively, contentedly. By this time, though, participants had taken the writing program for granted: "Of course it works. That's been obvious for some time."

TABLE 1

Mean Global Outcomes for Writers (N = 16) over the Six Stages of Treatment (bds = brief, daily sessions)

(Stages)	Motivation	Imagination	Fluency	Control	Audience	Resilience
Constancy (objective) (moderation) % bds on schedule	34%	42%	69%	68%	66%	73%
(abundance) productivity as pp./week	1.9	1.2	4.2	3.0	2.6	3.1
Comfort (subjective) (moderation) self-rate (1–10) pacing & outing	3.3	5.1	5.0	6.8	6.2	7.8
(abundance) self-rate (1–10) excitement & effort	6.5	5.9	4.4	4.5	5.8	3.5

Table 1 provoked most discussion about the waning of outputs and satisfactions for the maximized practices ("Yeah, maximizing has taken a back seat, for good reason. You can see that it doesn't work nearly so well as moderating"). Writers here most often reflected on advantages for moderation in writing with more clarity and with less fatigue: "I am reminded of something I once read, I can't remember where, of an aging, wiser writer saying he was writing more slowly, thus more economically, more clearly, better. Me too." Second on the list of advantages was the importance of moderation (cf. maximization) in bringing both constancy and productivity: "The steady accumulation, drip by drip by drip, is amazing; no pain and lots of gain". By this point, no one tried to make the exclusive case for bingeing at writing that had been so familiar at the program's outset.

Measures of Moderated Constancy for Brief Daily Sessions (Table 1)

Two things about brief, daily sessions for writing activities stood out: 1) The steady climb toward high levels of reliability and the surprising slowness of the climb; 2) The long wait in establishing a reliable habit of writing. Together, these two points elicited reflections about original expectations from almost all writers ("I honestly imagined I could get it in place in a few weeks"). But writers were ready with useful explanations ("OK, what I understand now is that writing has to be a truly ingrained habit; [it has to be] an automatic habit and that doesn't happen overnight").

From these discussions came a common inference. New faculty were, by the end of the writing program, almost universally convinced that this constancy was the most vital thing they had learned ("Nothing else is nearly as important to me. Why is that? Because, until you work at it every day you just don't get to be better at it…you just don't get it"). Writers also agreed that constancy was the most philosophically troubling thing to master ("For a long time, I hated it. I hated the forcing, and I was impatient and I wanted to do other things.…Eventually, though, I'll tell you, I stopped noticing the hassle. At some point, I'm not sure when, I started looking forward to my writing; the struggle was gone"). As a rule, writers were specific about what had been most important in instilling this constancy: the program ("At one time, you know, I thought I could do this on my own, but I doubt I would have. I still run across my original partner and she left [the group] with the same plan. She didn't stick with it for long").

Finally, Table 1 reminded writers of something in the literature about writing successes for novice professors: The earlier the installation of this habit, the better for careers (Creswell, 1985).

Global Measures of Maximized Constancy

Although I labeled writers' plans for maximizing as inefficient if overused, groups and I delighted in trying out excesses. (Writers need occasional respites from rules including mine.) In fact, occasional binges did not interfere with constancy or comfort when they allowed writers to maintain at least two brief daily sessions in any given week. Reportedly, there were profits in occasional respites from regular discipline ("It was a weekend where I buried myself in the manuscript. I needed to live it, breathe it, to see it clearly—how it went together").

Still, writers who had most wanted to maximize were startled by their eventual preference for brief daily sessions and for modest outputs—of only about a page per day (three to five days a week). How could so much less than initial ideals of maximizing (an output over 25 pp./wk. was deemed desirable) suffice? Part of the answer lay in original overestimates of how much would be enough. These new faculty were all from departments where norms for retention and tenure were the equivalent of 1.0 to 1.5 manuscripts per year in refereed journals. At a moderate rate of about a typed page per scheduled writing day (even with rewriting), usual outputs in the first year of participation in the program were 100 to 400 pages of patient, reflective, and revised scholarly prose.

For awhile, comments on the global data about maximizing continued to dominate conversations. Most of all, new faculty focused with near incredulity on the eventual productivity afforded by the moderation of brief daily sessions ("You probably remember that I so confidently stated that I couldn't get enough writing done with bds. Right? I said, I think, you can't do any worthwhile writing in a half-hour or hour. Before long I did, though"). Second, writers increasingly reflected on finally having appreciated the inefficiency of binges ("I was too burned out to write again for over a week"). They even asked to see more data. When Table 1 was broken down for individual analyses, the patterns showed that writers who most often wrote in binge sessions evidenced the lowest output and comfort levels over the long run. Third, writers looking at the global results talked about moderation as having taken pressures off writing, especially for quick successes ("tennis doesn't happen instantly and magically, so why should writing?"). And fourth, writers expressed satisfaction in faring better than peers who dropped out of the program ("so what more do we need to say: they wrote almost nothing this year, that they had less fun, hey?").

TRANSFERRING WRITERLY STRATEGIES TO TEACHING

I continued to provide formalized strategies and assessments for each stage in part two of the project. While I encouraged groups to expand their growing sense of flexibility in devising their programs, I cautioned them to stay in touch with original procedures for writing. Overall, groups closely approximated the scheme presented the year before for writing (here, we called them writerly rules for teaching—Boice, 1995b).

We, those of us who have braved the chapters above, already know the essential goals and measures.

ESSENTIAL OUTCOMES OF THE TEACHING PROGRAM

In part two, as in part one, analyses and redirections occurred periodically. Here too they peaked toward the end, as part of honing efforts that would help teachers persist beyond the program. First, we reset our perspective with an examination of what happened in part one.

Looking First for Links to the Writing Program

Another look at the writing data reminded teachers of the writerly scheme they were importing to teaching (normative comments: "You see, now it is showing up as clearly as can be…. What we were doing to help our writing seems obviously more general than just for writing"). Revisits to the sorts of data shown in Table 1 confirmed the sense of generality. And they prompted recognitions of savings: "Now I realize, I guess, how much easier this has been in the second year. We were much speedier this time because we were just redoing many of the same things that we already knew how to do").

"What happens to people who start out with teaching and then deal with writing next?" My answer to this common question was this: In shepherding 16 other new faculty through this reversed format (with failures for another three), part one moved more slowly for teaching than for writing. The reasons offered by stayers in the reversed program are not surprising: There is simply less incentive to work at teaching, especially so long as writing remains a problem. And, writerly principles do not seem fully convincing until they are first applied to writing.

Looking for Savings and Other Progress in the Teaching Program

Table 2 confirms the savings just mentioned in terms of global measures in part two. Compliance/reliability levels for brief sessions (called brief, daily sessions in part one) started at much higher percentages in part two. Clearly, these participants had quicker starts in part two than in part one. The surprise was that levels of constancy grew little higher over time. What most teachers (and writers) eventually judged as ideal were reliabilities around the three-quarters mark.

TABLE 2

Mean Global Outcomes for Teachers (N = 16) over the Six Stages of Treatment (bds = brief, daily sessions)

(Stages)	Motivation	Imagination	Fluency	Control	Audience	Resilience
Constancy (objective)						
% brief sessions on schedule	64%	72%	73%	85%	72%	84%
Comfort (subjective)						
self-rate (1-10) pacing & outing	6.6	8.0	8.0	8.1	6.4	8.8

Why? Because these new faculty, like the exemplars they modeled after, saw the need for moderation: "It gets to be a bore if I have to stick to the routines like a robot...besides, I don't need to do more. I'm doing fine now."

Individual Differences in Setting Optimal Levels of Constancy and Comfort

Some teachers (and writers) demanded higher and more stable elevations than others. Five of these 16 participants worked at levels of constancy that typically remained above 90%. Four showed similarly high levels of reliable practice, but in streaks. And seven settled into constancies that hovered around 60–70%.

Variable types. The pattern started early. By stage two (Imagination) of the writing program, new faculty who were the most variable practicers of exercises showed markedly less imagination, productivity, and comfort as writers. By the midpoint of part one, though, they offered justifications for lagging behind. Deliberately slow compliance enabled them to maintain a sense of what they talked about far more often than other writers: freedom and spontaneity (e.g., "I need to do this on *my* terms, in my own way"). However, they did report special value in finally learning to restrict their pessimism and pain as writers ("that's more important to me....That had to come first").

Compliants. Teachers almost always persisted in styles of compliance similar to what they had established as writers. New faculty in the highly compliant and reliable group reported taking special pleasure in having made customs of a difficult set of practices for both writing and teaching. Their comments about working at teaching paralleled what they had said as writers: "It's great because I don't have to wrestle with all these things. I do them because they are habits. They're good habits. And I like it because it makes me feel disciplined and smart."

What prices did these groups see themselves as having paid for their styles as participants? High compliants saw almost none, except for not having adopted brief daily sessions and other time-saving strategies sooner. They prided themselves, in comparison to other writers, for having made more progress at productivity and comfort ("But I don't think it was a competitive thing. I was doing it for myself when I was doing it. Now I'm just pleased to see how well I did, comparatively"). As teachers, high compliants could more readily specify their greater efficiencies (e.g., in terms of the ratio of time spent preparing vs. time in classes). They took singular pleasure at most closely adopting the habits and attitudes of new faculty labeled as exemplary. But, they chafed, usually privately, at the resentment that other participants sometimes expressed toward them ([She said to me:] "So, are you going to write a book extolling all your successes here?"). Perhaps the most impressive outcome for high compliants was their greater tendency to offer insights about the program and about interconnections of teaching and writing: "Once you see the real point of this, of getting more done in less time, you can make life a whole lot easier for yourself"; "I guess the most important thing I've learned is how wasteful it has been to think of teaching and writing as completely different things."

Moderate compliants. Compared to high compliants, moderate compliants continued to exhibit more negativism, cynicism, and pain about writing and teaching. In the groups, other teachers appreciated them for their ready humor ("The only constancy I can report is in the blank faces of my students"). Moderate compliants persisted in expecting writing and teaching to be hard work ("even though I see that maybe it doesn't have to be that way").

Variable compliants. The variable compliants were least involved in friendly banter. In groups, they spent more time than other participants expressing worries, busyness, and disapproval. They most often criticized program components that seemed regimented or quantitative. They most often accused colleagues of pessimism and authoritarianism (but, in my estimates, they were most likely to display both). In what may have been the ultimate test, variable types fared least well in terms of resiliency as teachers during stage six and in the year afterward. That is: They most often reported disturbing events. They most commonly experienced illnesses such as colds, flu, and insomnia.

Still, where they saw these outcomes as consequences of episodic compliance, variable types claimed to value their variability more than the costs:

> *Yes, I am often unhappier than the "compulsives" in the program....And I don't seem nearly so efficient. What I have that they don't have, I believe, are the real highs of getting back on track and the, um, dignity of knowing that I decided when to work. Don't forget that a lot of people become professors, poor salaries and all, to have this freedom....Don't forget that I am doing all right as a teacher and as a researcher. Students like*

> *me and I like them. I'm writing and publishing. I don't have to*
> *worry about tenure, I'm pretty sure.*

The program may have been more valuable to variable types than they would admit. It, after all, helped them improve their writing and teaching to acceptable levels. Moreover, variable types reported the most euphoria while managing compliance to the program: "I can't tell you how pleased I am." When they were freewheeling, variable types most often binged at work and other activities ("even shopping"). And then they most often reported distress at undoing their progress ("I guess I'm back to rushing and pressuring. My old anxieties are coming back").

Other Reflections by these Teachers

There were reaffirmations that dealing with disinterest and criticism (stage five) produces a drop in overall measures of program compliance and comfort ("I still hate to deal with it, but I'm getting better at it, at a tortoises's pace"). There was agreement that the early and late stages (e.g., motivation and resilience) added necessary length to a dauntingly long program ("Yeah, all that work on pacing and patience and efficiency was important;" "I understand now that these two years are not long at all, not in the scope of my career"). And there were emphatic expressions of fondness for the exercises on control ("And I didn't want anything to do with the psychological rituals at first").

Finally, teachers smiled in recollection of their original insistences on focusing improvements around intensity and excitement. This time the response was brief and ironic: "The question I want answered now is the same one that Joanna Field asked [in one of the readings for most program participants]: why did no one tell me these things about the importance of waiting before?"

Looking at Stage-Specific Experiences
in Teaching Improvement

What had at times seemed a mix of discrete exercises now fit together in ways most commonly labeled as "learning how to work" (Tremmel, 1989) or as "reflective practice" (Tremmel, 1993). That is, this basic sort of learning (of FOPs) could be seen to have expanded.

New faculty, once practicing habits of mindful work, often (N = 11) reported a new, scholarly curiosity about teaching excellence. Teachers who originally saw teaching as a nuisance now talked and read about it with some enthusiasm ("but don't get me wrong, I still am primarily a researcher").

Reasons now became clearer about why motivation exercises of patience, relaxation, and timing initially seemed so remote to new faculty struggling with teaching: "I just wanted help with my poor [student] ratings and I assumed that better ratings would be what I needed to feel more motivated. I was feeling very impatient right when you were harping about patience." Another thing about finding motivation had grown particularly clear: the value of practice in "slowing."

> *You know, this was a kind of conversion experience for me. I had originally thought that I could motivate my teaching by rushing, with intensity. You should have seen me. I was rushing to class, presenting a flurry of material, and walking out limp but congratulating myself on being a hard worker. Or consoling myself. I knew, for all that, that it wasn't working, and I didn't know why. I somehow thought I had to work even harder. And I did. The change came when I slowed down. I went to class early, as per prescription, and I took my time. I paused and so on. And I felt myself letting go of a lot of tension and impatience. I finally got it in two steps, I think. Finally I started to remember what I had learned about writing and, somewhat belatedly, to apply that sort of calm to teaching. Not long after, I realized I was starting class and I was relaxed and smiling, sort of beaming myself out onto the class, and I noticed that quite a few of the students were relaxed and smiling. And I thought, by God, I'm actually going to like doing this. It has been different, very different, since.*

Most new faculty in the program could recall a similar moment where exercises for motivation began to work. As a rule, this change accompanied an appreciation for brief sessions. Teachers could also remember their self-ratings of comfort going up at about the same time. Reports with the most feeling were about finding both discipline and freedom:

> *. . . see if I can make sense of this for you. It's taken me awhile to figure it out for myself. What happened first was the automatic habit, and that was comforting, but there was more to it than that. When the slowed pacing had become a habit and I had finally calmed down, I liked feeling more disciplined....What I hadn't noticed right away was that I also felt more in control of my pacing...I was not only slowing*

> *down more, but I was varying it more. What I really liked was*
> *when I speeded up at times on purpose…to wake them up.*
> *What I liked the most was realizing that I had gained some dis-*
> *cipline without becoming a mechanical teacher.*

Fluency exercises produced a similar path of experiences. Here too, everyone had struggled with constancy. Fourteen of the sixteen teachers reported that their acceptance of brief sessions developed with disappointing slowness. But a conscious sense of the worth of working regularly at teaching did come eventually, inevitably ("or was it just the habit, at last ingrained?" one teacher said in a note to me). Why had it been resisted for so long? Most participants now had answers ready in mind: They had placed what now seemed a surprisingly high value on writing with brilliance and magic, without constraints like schedules or rules ("I hate to be on any kind of plan or timetable"). They had insisted that work at teaching improvement be sporadic and spontaneous ("It was [like this]: [I work] when I'm in the mood for that sort of thing…but not *every* day").

Teachers liked to recall where this new habit became prominent. Before that point, participants remembered grudgingly practiced exercises. After, as the acts became more automatic, as routines proved more helpful, constancy became more agreeable ("I noticed it was feeling good, that I looked forward to these little times"). More important, regular practice had become desirable for its economy:

> *Look, this is what matters. It takes less time. It gets more done.*
> *It's simple, simple, simple. I end up with more time for myself.*
> *I'm not the slave to habit I worried about becoming. If any-*
> *thing, I'm becoming a slave to having more free time to do*
> *other things, like taking my dog for long walks. Maybe I'm*
> *fooling myself; I don't think so. I don't spend all that much*
> *time on either writing or teaching. I'm doing better at both.*
> *The only question I have is why this [program] isn't more*
> *widely used?*

Most important, participants reported, was the confidence that had emerged at about the same time:

> *There was moment where I unexpectedly felt like a teacher. I*
> *think it was because I had become a professional. I was work-*
> *ing efficiently at my practice, and I was getting better at being*
> *prepared and at presenting. Much more skilled, much more*
> *efficient. I felt more confident do you know? I felt unpressured*
> *to do the things that were making me a better teacher, and I*

was doing them anyway and that gave me a shot of confidence....There was a proud moment when I was in class and I found myself listening to myself and I pretty much thought, "I am saying things well, I'm doing this with ease; I am a good teacher!" That was a turning point, one that I believe came from regular practice more than anything.

Participants hung onto to this discussion longest, wondering again why the struggle for regimen and fluency (stage three) had proven so difficult, why it had demanded the most relearning of what had been mastered in part one. Some answers seemed superficial but may not have been: "I knew it, but I didn't know it. I had to see all over again how regular practice helped in teaching." Some seemed at last to admit to a general dilemma of writers and teachers:

Well, this is how I think it is. We don't ordinarily learn efficient ways to be professors. What we learn, I think, is to value autonomy and academic freedom. We learn to be suspicious of things like efficiencies, of formulas and so on....And we don't know how to be patient. We haven't been taught the value of good habits.

Curiously, the fifth stage, where teachers had made slow progress and experienced the most pain, elicited the least conversation. Part of the reason was that here, more than for any other stage, participants remained unsatisfied with their progress: "I know what I need to do and I'm tired of carping about it. It just needs more doing and less talking."

Resilience exercises produced the most reflection about growth as teachers, and for good reason. By definition they prompted teachers to study and reinvent themselves, to compare their progress with co-journeyers, and to anticipate problems ahead. The realizations they judged as most useful were linked to systematic ratings and notes. Two examples:

1. *Maybe a highlight of my day is making my few notes about what I have done well. It's time for myself. This is what I do: I often see signs there of progress in things like not getting off track in class...or staying with the really important problems in my manuscripts. Why this is so pleasing is that it's an account of progress. It is about someone making a good start in her career who will do even better. It's a nice story.*

2. *I make a few notes every day but mostly about my teaching. My writing speaks for itself and it carries itself. Teaching needs more cultivating, I*

think; I haven't been in the habit of thinking pleasant, inventive things about teaching. Not until now.

By the time participants routinely told me they were experiencing a new-found resilience, they were better at listing its specifics. They reported working with less moodiness, with less overreaction, with less surprise: "My work is steady. I feel like a rock. I can see problems coming, and I weather most of them better than I ever did." "The stronger my good habits, the better I stay on course."

In particular, teachers evaluating the reasons for their resilience took pride in seeing the simplicity of their accomplishments: "It really *is* nothing but constancy and comfort that we have been practicing. Of course you (nodding toward me) have been saying it all along. Yes?" They also liked pointing out how well the simplest of ideas applied back to their writing: "Do you know what? There are so many things about teaching that work for writing. What is just beginning to dawn on me is that I don't have to work so long, so hard, to do my best for myself, to do my best for my students."

DISCUSSION

Early readers supposed this the most conspicuous result of the program: that such basic mechanisms (FOPs) as patience can help writers and teachers. A second salient outcome is systematic, enduring evidence of broad-based change for faculty participants, something unusual in a field of faculty development where methods are rarely proven effective (Weimer & Lenze, 1991). And a third result is a demonstration that a developmental project can work to enrich both teaching and scholarly writing in the same faculty members.

Subtle Interventions and Changes

Onlookers came to appreciate subtle changes in the program when they examined participants' notes (and my own notes of participants' comments and recollections). In our discussions, I mentioned parallels from cognitive science to help make sense of outcomes.

Finding motivation. Salient interventions for finding motivation entailed waiting and relaxing. More covert changes relied on questioning inefficient beliefs (e.g., that the best motivation awaits the proper mood, preferably one of compelling urgency or easy magic). And motivation evidently arrived with repeated realizations of what was effective: beginning before feeling fully ready, writing and teaching in brief sessions, and moderating fatigue with deliberate pacing.

But according to participants in the program, motivation really shifted into gear when its discipline brought freedom. Writers, for example, reported feeling most enthusiastic about writing once daily portions could be completed quickly (and once brief daily sessions could be seen as sufficient to meet output needs). The point was not the mere saving in time; it was more the time available for other, unplanned things. For new faculty who self-rated their motivation highest, those other things were commonly associated with play.

Cognitive science makes a related point. Researchers on problem solving continue to struggle with ways of arranging motivation for students (Sternberg, 1985), but the best-informed guesses are that playfulness (i.e., working without immediate goals or ends in mind), constancy, and social support may be keys (Bruner, 1985). When we play, we rarely glaze over, drop out, or become fixated. And, play is generative. It encourages the recruitment of materials, of practice arrangements, of playmates, and of durable motivation.

Finding imagination. Here too, a key act was waiting (while delaying closure). Patient, proactive waiting promoted more play and discovery (via collecting, filing, rearranging, and conceptual outlining). It also elicited more awareness of why writers and teachers need to become immersed in the normal conversations of their genres (in part by listening; in part by beginning to share ideas/plans before feeling ready). Experts on problem solving remind us of a sound reason why this emphasis on "writing before writing" (and on teaching before teaching) works: It distributes the usual cognitive load over time, away from usual, concentrated practices of trying to think of what to say and to say it at the same time. Efficiency (i.e., intelligent action) is a matter of resource allocation (Perkins, 1985). Intelligence *is* efficiency.

Finding fluency. Prominent changes in learning fluency exemplified constancy and comfort. Writers, even teachers, mastered a habit of regular but usually brief periods of work at their craft. With that visible habitualness came a more private sense of competence and confidence, of ease in writing and saying. One common insight of program participants is that fluency, managed well, is more than productivity. It includes the moderation of not trying to do too much. It needs the planfulness of not trying to solve unnecessary problems, the self-control of not working too impulsively.

The literature on fostering intelligence suggests, again, that good thinkers show balance (Baron, 1985). They neither search too much nor too little. They benefit from training to be less impulsive (i.e., to take enough time and to make fewer errors). Research on the thought patterns behind impulsive behavior makes a related point: Dysfluencies often take root in unrealistic plans and standards. When actions fall short of perfection, overreaction and its emotional distress lead to bingeing and uncritical acceptance of irrational beliefs (Heatherton & Baumeister, 1991). Among those maladaptive tendencies is an irrational preference for working at writing and teaching only when conditions seem ideal. The result is sporadic, hurried, painful, inefficient work (Boice, 1994).

Finding control. Some of the most visible basics of the fourth stage, control, involved environmental rearrangements (e.g., setting up comforting surrounds that ensured moderate distractions). Somewhat less visible basics were matters of working on self-control (e.g., exercises of talking aloud to find rationality and mild happiness while working). Three private strategies of moderation in teaching were judged equally important: tempering the near mania of hypomania; suspending perfectionism until proofing and revising (because the delays give writers more time to be tentative, playful); limiting overattachment to content (and its kin, overreaction to criticism). Teachers of thinking, including cognitive therapists, make a similar point: impulsives can be helped when they learn to pace and space their actions (Bruer, 1993).

Finding audience. The most publicly-valued act of audience proved to be externalizing—putting thoughts outward in ways that allowed teachers to understand and be understood. Appreciation of other, more subtle changes came more slowly for a sense of audience than in any other stage. What emerged eventually was an awareness of a crucial kind of tolerance, one that permits a great letting-go: Allowing others to do some of the work of writing and teaching. This loosening-up seems to educate writers and teachers about patience, playfulness, and even social sophistication. It apparently facilitates a related kind of tolerance so covert that few participants recognized it at first. A thoroughly educated, socially skilled sense of audience requires a tolerance that helps writers and teachers interpret correction as feedback, not as opposition (Bruner, 1985). As participants found criticism more tolerable, they grew more tolerant of differences in how other people wrote or taught.

Finding resilience. Basic skills of resilience were, by nature, mostly private. What had been a program of following and adapting publicly shared regimens became one of self-study and self-reinvention to improve efficiencies in work. The same old principles—constancy and control—continued to be essential; what changed was the stance. It more often became futuristic, one of looking ahead so as to weather likely storms. There were usually unspoken goals in this: to permit more variability in expectations and more tolerance of failings ("Now I'm learning that just doing something, not everything, on a bad day, is what counts"). The most private of these private experiences reportedly occurred when writers and teachers began to reinvent themselves (even their personalities) as teachers:

> *I like the new image I have of myself. In the classroom, I'm outgoing, smiling, patient. Not worried about being perfect; I'm there to share my careful preparations and my considerable expertise; I'm there with a genuine interest to see what works and what doesn't. In a way it's like the way I once saw myself, in slow motion, when I became a pretty good volley ball player. I can tell you, it isn't some pipe dream. It is already happening....[In response to my question: What has it to do with resilience?] Everything. To get past the moment, past whatever thing is bad now, I need that image of myself moving on to more successes.*

This resilience, too, has parallels in other research: Again, efficiency (particularly in allocating resources) matters (Sternberg, 1985). And, to ensure resilience, we need to constantly remind ourselves why the best problem solving strategies often become inoperative: we forget them; we use them in ways that produce an unpleasant cognitive load; we irrationally reject them as implausible or as unneeded; and we let their definitions and practices drift from their original meanings (Perkins, 1985).

With questions answered about what changes occur to writers and teachers in the program, tougher ones come up.

How Do I Know Writing and Teaching Really Improved?

This hard question reflects skepticism with some of the unconventional measures of progress I use. Onlookers offered few qualms about indexing writing productivity in terms of verified outputs of pages per work week. (Although queries arose about how completely productivity translates into publishability.) But academics are not unused to gauging progress as teachers (or as writers) in terms like setting and carrying out plans for pacing work. Onlookers expressed even more doubt about the value of self-rated comfort for tasks like limiting classroom preparations and welcoming criticism.

Answers that help assuage these reservations are not hard to come by and should, arguably, be part of any teaching improvement program. First, I note, there is tangible evidence of progress in the measures already provided. The outcomes reflect goals consistent with the advice of experts in teaching improvement (e.g., interact more with students; solicit more feedback). And the data do show gradual but real successes in meeting those goals of constancy and comfort (e.g., slowed pace and more efficiency in presenting crucial ideas; more acceptance of help and criticism). Moreover, the results differ in expected ways from control data.

Controls. A matched control group of 16 new faculty who did not participate in the program (they considered themselves on a waiting list to participate later) agreed to respond to my monthly calls with accounts and ratings like those completed by participating colleagues. Controls were not difficult to recruit ("Why not? I may get something from it, and I don't have to do much"). They often supposed that occasional attention to the program, even from a distance, might help them as writers and teachers ("I'm not in the program yet, but I am trying to follow a schedule of brief, daily work"). Over time, they seemed insightful about why their marginal participation produced little change from what they had already been doing ("Maybe the group meetings and having to report what everyone is doing would make me do the things I should?").

In the end, controls' measures remained essentially unchanged from beginning levels (or from a close similarity to the initial data for full participants). My other studies of far larger samples of new faculty, often over longer periods, indicate that without strong, persistent help for work habits and social supports, most new faculty perform at disappointing levels (Boice, 1992b; 1993a). In the absence of programmatic help, only exemplars truly thrive during early, formative years (and even they find lots of help).

My second response to skeptics relies on more readily acceptable measures. Compared to the controls just mentioned, these 16 participants showed clear progress in four domains:

1. They more often completed at least one scholarly manuscript per year (75% for participants vs. 19% for controls in Year 1; 94% vs. 25% in Year 2).

2. They more often had manuscripts accepted for publication in a refereed, scholarly medium (38% vs. 6% in Year 1; 63% vs. 25% through Year 2).

3. They managed more improvements in scores on standardized, end-of-semester evaluations by students in their classes:

   Year 1 rating = 2.4 vs. 2.0 (cf. a campus mean of 2.3 for the item used as a global index—"I would recommend this class to a friend"; higher numerical ratings are more desirable; comparisons were limited to undergraduate classes only).

   Year 2 rating = 3.0 vs. 2.2 (vs. same global item).

   An added note: these increases in student ratings came in the wake of moderated time spent preparing for classes. Exemplars consistently show the same economy (Boice, 1992b).

4. Full participants were far more likely to have received specific approval of their progress as writers and as teachers from colleagues in their retention/tenure committees (38% vs. 13% in Year 1; 75% vs. 19% in Year 2). These new faculty were thriving, and their colleagues noticed it.

My third general answer about the reality of change for participants seems trivial to onlookers, but only initially. Program graduates supposed (and I agreed) that a good index of progress is the extent to which they became mentors or coaches for other new faculty. All 16, some sooner and more thoroughly, assumed this teacherly role of working with junior colleagues. Most of the mentors' remarks to me followed an already familiar pattern (e.g., teaching as a way to relearn writerly principles). Only five participants, those most involved in mentoring, mentioned its importance to the campus ("You must already know this; I've just figured it. The only way this program can reach many of the new people is for graduates to become developers").

The closing question came from onlookers who remained unconvinced.

Does This Approach Leave Any Room for Art in Writing and Teaching?

Skeptics (and some have been hostile) often interpret my approach as too formulaic, too rational to help writers and teachers develop individual, creative styles. I would do better, I am told, to rely less on data and to promote reflective practice, an approach that disdains linear, rule-bound steps for improving teaching because it is a holistic act of knowing-in-action, of adapting insights to bear on what we do not know.

But even this "humanistic" alternative, I believe, has links to the writerly ways presented here. FOPs mean paying attention to what matters in the moment, to habits of mind and matters of feeling. They mean awareness of real choices made along the way, of freedom that begins with moderate and flexible discipline. They mean a smooth, free thinking way of observing, discovering, adjusting (Tremmel, 1993).

Writerly ways are in fact reflective practices. They focus on process (not product). They have enjoyable steps and rules. They come down to simple and recursive acts of patience and tolerance. And while writerly ways do offer generalized solutions, they encourage far greater freedom of expression and time than new faculty experience without the program.

What the Real Objection May Be

FOPs require lots of practice. They require basic changes. They require a long-term investment.

To prime you to continue this journey, I draw out some simple, memorable lessons as examples of the lessons you might look for later, in other reading and experience. Happy trails to you!

References

Baron, J. (1985). What kinds of intelligence components are fundamental? In S.F. Chipman & J.W. Segal (Eds.), *Thinking and Learning Skills*, vol. 2. Hillsdale, NJ: Erlbaum, 365-390.

Baumeister, R.F., & Scher, S.F. (1988). Self-defeating behavior patterns among normal individuals: Review and analysis of common self-destructive tendencies. *Psychological Review 104*, 3-22.

Beck, A.T., Rush, J.A., Shaw, B.F., & Emery, G. (1979). *Cognitive therapy of depression*. New York, NY: Guilford.

Bluedorn, A.C., Kaufman, C.F., & Lane, P.M. (1992). How many things do you like to do at once? An introduction to monochronic and polychronic time. *Academy of Management Executive 6*: 17-26.

Boice, R. (1989). Procrastination, busyness, and bingeing. *Behaviour Research & Therapy 27*: 605- 611.

Boice, R. (1991). Quick starters. *New Directions for Teaching and Learning 48*, 111-121.

Boice, R. (1992a). Combined treatments for writing blocks. *Behaviour Research & Therapy 30*: 107-116.

Boice, R. (1992b). *The new faculty member*. San Francisco, CA: Jossey-Bass.

Boice, R. (1993a). New faculty involvement for women and minorities. *Research in Higher Education 34*, 291-341.

Boice, R. (1993b). Primal origins of midcareer disillusionment. *New Directions for Teaching and Learning 55*, 33-41.

Boice, R. (1993c). Writing blocks and tacit knowledge. *Journal of Higher Education 64*: 19-54.

Boice, R. (1994). *How writers journey to fluency and comfort: A psychological adventure*. New York, NY: Praeger.

Boice, R. (1995a). Developing writing, then teaching amongst new faculty. *Research in Higher Education 36*, 415-456.

Boice, R. (1995b). Writerly rules for teaching. *Journal of Higher Education 66*, 32-60.

Boyer, E.L. (1990). *Scholarship reconsidered*. Princeton, NJ: Carnegie Foundation.

Boyle, P. (1996). *Developmental socialization experiences of new graduate students.* Dissertation, State University of New York at Stony Brook.

Brand, A.G. (1989). *The psychology of writing: The affective experience.* Westport, CT: Greenwood.

Braxton, J.H., & Bayer, A.E. (1986). Assessing faculty scholarly performance. *New Directions for Institutional Research 50,* 25-42.

Bruer, J.T. (1993). The mind's journey from novice to expert. *American Educator 17*(2), 6-15 & 38- 46.

Bruner, J. (1985). On teaching thinking. In S.F. Chipman & J.W. Segal (Eds.), *Teaching and Learning Skills,* vol. 2. Hillsdale, NJ: Erlbaum, 597-608.

Bullough, R.V., Knowles, J.G., & Crow, N.A. (1991). *Emerging as a teacher.* New York, NY: Routledge.

Covey, S.R. (1989). *The seven habits of highly effective people.* New York, NY: Fireside.

Creswell, J.W. (1985). *Faculty research performance.* Washington, DC: Association for the Study of Higher Education.

Eisenberger, R. (1992). Learned industriousness. *Psychological Review 99*: 248-267.

Eison, J. (1991). Confidence in the Classroom: Ten maxims for new teachers. *College Teaching 38*: 21-25.

Elbow, P. (1992). Freewriting and the problem of wheat and tares. In J. Moxley (Ed.), *Writing and publishing for academic authors.* Lanham, MD: University Press of America, 33-47.

Ellis, A., & Knaus, W.J. (1977). *Overcoming procrastination.* New York, NY: Institute for Rational Living.

Fairweather, J.S. (1993). Academic values and faculty rewards. *Review of Higher Education 17,* 43- 68.

Field, J. (1981). *A life of one's own.* Los Angeles, CA: J.P. Tarcher (Originally published 1936).

Flower, L. (1990). The role of task representation in reading-to-write. In L. Flower, V. Stein, J. Ackerman, M.J. Kantz, K. McCormick, & W.C. Peck (Eds.), *Reading to write.* New York, NY: Oxford University Press, 35-75.

Flower, L., & Hayes, J.R. (1981). Plans that guide the composing process. In C.H. Frederiksen & J.F. Dominic (Eds.), *Writing: The nature, development, and teaching of written communication.* Hillsdale, NJ: Erlbaum, 39-58.

Heatherton, T.F., & Baumeister, R.F. (1991). Binge eating as escape from self-awareness. *Psychological Bulletin 110,* 86-108.

Ingram, R. (1990). Self-focused attention in clinical disorders: Review and a conceptual model. *Psychological Bulletin 107,* 156-176.

James, W. (1898). *Talks to teachers.* New York, NY: Henry Holt.

Jamison, K.R. (1993). *Touched with fire.* New York, NY: Free Press.

Kearney, P., & Plax, T.G. (1992). Student resistance to control. In V.P. Richmond & J.C. McCroskey (Eds.), *Power in the classroom.* Hillsdale, NJ: Erlbaum, 85-99.

Kuiper, N.A., Olinger, L.J., & Martin, R.A. (1988). Dysfunctional attitudes, stress, and negative emotions. *Cognitive Therapy and Research 12,* 533-547.

Langer, E.J. (1989). *Mindfulness.* Reading, MA: Addison-Wesley.

Logue, A.W. (1994). *Self-control.* Englewood Cliffs, NJ: Prentice-Hall.

McCaul, K.D., Glasgow, R.E., & O'Neill, H.K. (1992). The problem of creating habits: Establishing health-protective dental behaviors. *Health Psychology:* 101-111.

McKeachie, W.J. (1994). *Teaching tips,* 9/e. Lexington, MA: D.C. Heath.

Mills, C.W. (1959). *The sociological imagination.* New York, NY: Grove Press.

Murray, D.M. (1978). Write before writing. *College Composition and Communication 29,* 375-381.

Oatley, K., & Jenkins, J.M. (1992). Human emotions: Function and dysfunction. *Annual Review of Psychology 43,* 55-85.

Olson, G.A. (1992). Publishing scholarship in humanistic disciplines: Joining the conversation. In J.M. Moxley (Ed.), *Writing and publishing for academic authors.* Lanham, MD: University Press of America, 49-69.

Pace, C.R. (1987). *Good things go together.* Los Angeles, CA: Center for the Study of Evaluation, University of California.

Perkins, D.N. (1981). *The mind's best work.* Cambridge, MA: Harvard University Press.

Perkins, D.N. (1985). General cognitive skills: Why not? In S.F. Chipman & J.W. Segal (Eds.), *Thinking and learning skills,* vol. 2. Hillsdale, NJ: Erlbaum, 339- 363.

Perkins, D. (1993). Teaching for understanding. *American Educator* 17(3), 8, 28-35.

Rice, R.E. (1992). The new American scholar: Scholarship and the purposes of the university. *Metropolitan Universities 1,* 7-18.

Richlin, L. (1993). To hear all voices: A broader view of faculty scholarship. *New Directions for Teaching and Learning 54,* 39-46.

Ronkowski, S.A. (1993). Scholarly teaching: Developmental stages of pedagogical scholarship. *New Directions for Teaching and Learning 54,* 79-90.

Scardamalia, M., & Bereiter, C. (1985). Fostering the development of self-regulation in children's knowledge processing. In S.F. Chipman & J.W. Segal (Eds.), *Thinking and Learning Skills,* vol. 2. Hillsdale, NJ: Erlbaum, 563-577.

Skinner, B.F. (1971). *Beyond freedom and dignity.* New York, NY: Knopf.

Sternberg, R.J. (1985). Instrumental and componential approaches to the nature and training of intelligence. In S.F. Chipman & J.W. Segal (Eds.), *Thinking and Learning Skills,* vol. 2. Hillsdale, NJ: Erlbaum, 215-243.

Strunk, W., & White, E.B. (1979). *The elements of style.* New York, NY: Macmillan.

Tremmel, R. (1989). Investigating productivity and other factors in the writer's practice. *Freshman English News* 17(2), 19-25.

Tremmel, R. (1993). Zen and the art of reflective practice in teacher education. *Harvard Educational Review 63,* 434-438.

Weimer, M. (1990). *Improving college teaching.* San Francisco, CA: Jossey-Bass.

Weimer, M.G., & Lenze, L.F. (1991). Instructional interventions: A review of the literature on efforts to improve instruction. In J.C. Smart (Ed.), *Higher education: Handbook of theory and research.* New York, NY: Agathon, 294-333.

PART II

Metacognitions About FOPs for Teaching

Lesson One: Recognize Society's Real Objections to Efficiencies

Consider, first of all, that our schools and advice books say little about learning ways to work efficiently. Clearly, we are unaccustomed to examining the topic. Why?

MAGICAL BELIEFS ABOUT GENIUS AND CREATIVITY

Myths about teachers who seemingly produce brilliant classes with little work, or better yet by way of divine inspiration, are attractive; they make teaching seem a special talent or gift. These myths are enormously reinforcing to some teachers who use them to project genius and mysticism. Tradition, it seems, has no reason to give up faith in magic and sudden genius in favor of more realistic, proven ways of working.

Teachers already working with success and audience are most often in a position to change that tradition, but they may have no objection to the continuing failures of most colleagues as teachers. They can (and do) dismiss inefficient teachers as untalented and ungifted.

Even teachers who do not teach fluently or happily often help encourage this tradition of social Darwinism. If they do not excel, they can take comfort in the belief that they lack only the blessing of the Muses or the right genes. In my experience, teachers who try but fail are the *most* likely to suppose that good teaching must reflect magic and genius, not hard work. These attitudes leave them unlikely to seek or accept help, to adopt efficiencies, or to think well of those of us who do. The irony is that teachers who need them most are least interested in learning efficiencies.

EFFICIENCIES AS EMBARRASSING, SOCIALLY IMPOLITE

The myths and beliefs we just saw create another problem: Silence or suppression. Conversation (or writing) about efficiencies is embarrassing, almost taboo in academe. We might sooner talk about our sexual dysfunctions than our teaching inefficiencies. Why? Because inefficiencies can imply a failure of will or character. Because their discussion with a sufferer can be embarrassing. Because practices of efficiencies may be seen as admissions of low intelligence.

One more thing discourages widespread use of economies of working. Systems of efficiency are disparaged on the assumption (unproven) that they necessarily make teachers miserable, unimaginative, and superficial. For all these reasons, most teachers who write for other teachers graciously avoid the uncomfortable topic of working efficiently. When they mention the usual problems of inefficiencies at all, notably procrastination and blocking, they treat them lightly, politely, humorously:

> *The Law of Delay: That which can be delayed, will be.*
> Donald Murray

EFFICIENCIES AS TACIT KNOWLEDGE

Because efficiencies seem necessary only for those who cannot succeed without help, we tend to keep them unstated and generally unknown (i.e., tacit). And vague. And hard to teach. And hard to consider as generally necessary or socially acceptable.

Research on children who ordinarily fail at school helps show why tacit knowledge is important. Without the skills that characterize exemplary students (e.g., knowing how and when to talk in class; how to study; how to find social supports), at-risk students are seen as lacking a vaguely defined quality called talent. But when naive students are taught these usually tacit skills of efficiency, their performance improves almost immediately. (Learning how to work is as important for success at school as at teaching school.) Why, then, don't teachers traditionally teach these tacit skills for success in school? They are unaccustomed to doing so (and the doing might seem like pandering). They are content with a system where some students (seemingly the most intelligent and the most like them) come to class prepared to learn quickly, with a minimum of direct help. They, like the rest of us, reserve special admiration for students who show brilliance under situations with incomplete information and sporadic supports. (And, after all, the teachers themselves have survived and excelled in traditional academic culture.)

Research on expertise makes a similar point about the shortcoming of traditional beliefs. Talent is probably not an inborn potential. Writers, musicians, and artists *all* must work hard, regularly, and efficiently to attain expertise. (So too, presumably, teachers.) To learn the usually tacit knowledge of efficiency, all of them rely on master teachers and broad social contacts (even critics).

To suppose that college teachers must learn on their own (preferably to work quickly, brilliantly, privately), is to ignore the facts. What ordinarily keeps us from ready access to this information and teaching is little more than the short-sighted, elitist belief that only "gifted" people can teach well. Or that only ungifted, immodest people would concern themselves with efficiency. Pride is the friend of perfectionism...and the enemy of efficiency.

EFFICIENCIES SEEN AS THREATS TO FREEDOM AND CREATIVITY

Earlier we saw traditional notions that efficiency and freedom are incompatible. They are so pervasive and persistent that they merit a quick disputation here.

Why do teachers, in fact, find more freedom and spontaneity once practicing efficiencies? Efficient teachers create more free time. They experiment, playfully and joyfully, with more alternatives for seeing and doing. They build imagination and self-esteem (while shedding the constraints of perfectionism and elitism). And they stop struggling to work at teaching, even when faced with disruptions. This is why writers who work in brief daily sessions produce more writing, better quality writing, and more creative writing than do counterparts who work spontaneously, only when in the mood. And it is why teachers who practice similar FOPs garner higher ratings, even better student note taking.

In sum, I know of no factual, reasonable arguments against efficiencies practiced with moderation and balance. Efficiencies deserve a patient, tolerant try.

Lesson Two: The Key Elements of Efficiency are Pacing and Exteriorizing

Taken together, the ten rules for efficiency have two common themes. For one thing, they amount to calming and slowing (with varied rhythms and punctuations of rest and excitement). For another, they mean putting more of the work of writing and teaching outside your head (onto paper/screen or into conversation). In their simplest form, these two factors can be called pacing and exteriorizing.

PACING

This, as you may recall, begins with patience. It includes reflection, even time for active waiting and its preplanning and prewriting/preteaching. It requires skills of timely stopping and of monitoring for emotions and thoughts that disrupt or exaggerate pacing. Efficient pacing is most fundamentally a matter of working in a process mode—as opposed to a product orientation.

Process styles generally keep us oriented to the work of the moment, to mindful awareness of our actions and decisions as work is ongoing. Its present-orientation helps to minimize ruminations about past failures and to limit thoughts of the future to what we want to accomplish now (not to anxieties about possible failures and injustices). When we work largely in the moment, we tend to proceed more calmly and patiently, with better imagination and problem solving. When we get past the impatience that usually makes process modes intolerable, we work with more willingness to listen, change, and revise—with more constancy and stronger habits, and with more resilience.

What, again, keeps most teachers and writers from working in this delightful, efficient state of pacing? Impatience and intolerance.

EXTERIORIZING

Exteriorizing is an odd word. It refers to the efficient act of putting ideas for writing and teaching outside our minds. The sooner the better. Why? Personal speech is cryptic and unstable, sometimes not even verbal. The more quickly we translate it into broadly understood and consistent messages, the more readily and fluently we can understand it and teach it. Writing and preparing in our heads are possible, but writing and thinking on paper or screen are far more efficient. Once we are "externalizing," we learn what we have to say, we stimulate new thoughts, and make more tangible progress toward fluent speech and prose.

We first saw exteriorizing as the essence of beginning early (rule two). It admonishes teachers to move beyond the usual preference of merely thinking about a project to actually putting ideas and plans outward: as talking aloud to oneself and to others; as freewriting and conceptual outlining before fully knowing what is going to be said. This initial kind of externalizing works because it establishes two worthwhile outcomes: The first is early momentum and approximations of plans that grow into motivation, imagination, and easy transitions to formal speaking and writing. (That is, motivation and imagination begin most reliably from the outside.) And exteriorizing's second advantage lies in doing something else that implicit, private thinking cannot do well: It helps us discover and clarify and expand our thoughts in the generally linear, logical fashion necessary for most teaching and writing.

> *How do I know what I think until I hear what I say?*
> William James

How do I know what I think until I see what I write?
Old saying by composition teachers

Exteriorizing practiced in the intermediate rules consisted of the deliberate monitoring in charting and displaying our progress against plans. It was also a part of noticing maladaptive thought patterns by talking them aloud, by disputing and replacing them aloud. It was an essential part of getting in touch with the emotions that accompany our work at writing; by noticing and noting their presence and effects, we gained more control over our teaching and writing. Curiously, all forms of exteriorizing are about gaining control—by first giving up some familiar controls.

To gain control, you must first give it up.
Ancient Zen maxim

Exteriorizing as we practiced it somewhat later helped as a more social act. It includes sharing early materials with critics and letting others do some of the work (rule nine) as a means of making teaching and writing more socially acceptable and more efficient, even of moderating the attachments to content that cause narrowness and overreaction (rule eight). Externalizing is also about letting go (and eventually finding a greater sense of control and self-esteem). And it too is about the tolerance, particularly of the criticism and failure that comes with externalizing, that helps build resilience.

Said another way, pacing and exteriorizing (and all the rules that expand on their meanings and practices) are really nothing but patience and tolerance. These two qualities may be the most essential outcomes of education in general.

Lesson Three:
To Master Efficiencies, Practice Them in Other Domains

You might suppose that teaching and writing are domain-specific talents, acts unlike each other or any other. Teaching, after all, seems to involve unique ways of thinking and expressing. Evidently, experienced and successful teachers and writers actually store whole patterns for solving problems in their memories. They know complicated, effective strategies for conjuring beginnings, revising, and so on. All they need to do (often unconsciously) is to call up the right programs. This is why practice and its expertise promote efficiency.

Still, some of the most fundamental ways of working economically and comfortably at teaching (and writing) generalize to other tasks. We already know one proven extension, to sleeping efficiently. When we practice the same basic rules in other domains, the strategies for working efficiently remain much the same. For instance, when I lived in a mountain cabin I learned to make the task of cutting and splitting eight cords of firewood each year more efficient in many of the same ways I had learned to work as a writer and teacher. I didn't rush into it (or, like most of my neighbors, procrastinate until the last minute, when the wood couldn't be properly seasoned before burning it). I took time to prepare by picking the trees carefully (much as a forestry agent had advised me to in promoting the health of my woods). Then, long before I needed to begin, I began the work in brief daily sessions, as breaks from my writing and reading. In a single 15–30 minute session I could fell a tree, or delimb it, or section it, or cart several pieces to my splitting station, and so on. I was disciplined about pausing and stopping while working (lumberjacking is an activity that tempts me to keep going). So I managed a process orientation of working in the present (a good safety measure in tasks like chainsawing that imperil daydreamers) while attending to my pleasant thoughts, emotions, and observations (my dog never seemed more content than when watching me work). I let others do some of the work (when I could). And I grew more resilient at wood cutting/splitting. Two things stood out when I finished my wood piles each year. I had finished early and had no worries about my heat supply for the coming winter. I enjoyed the work (unlike my neighbors who claimed to hate the task). Finishing early and efficiently provided a special sense of pride and freedom.

I can't prove that exporting the efficiencies of writing and teaching to wood cutting made me better at all three. It seemed that way. But I do have evidence (see Chapter 11) that applying these basic efficiencies to both teaching and writing leads to more improvement in either realm than practicing just one. Why does generalizing help? It requires clarification and simplification of the rules to apply them to a new domain. Successes in one stimulate enthusiasm and confidence for persisting with rules in the other. Successes can be seen to depend far more on learning and practicing a few basics (e.g., patience and tolerance) than on having to master large sets of separate problem solving strategies. And, most important, generalizing basic ways of working helps produce the insight that teaching is not so separate an endeavor as we often suppose.

Once teachers appreciate the role of efficiencies in their work, they realize that teaching relies heavily on a few learnable skills. And when they put aside talent notions about teaching excellence in favor of beliefs that its skills can be taught and learned, they assume a much more optimistic stance about being able to become better teachers

To a limited extent then,...we come into a position to steer a little bit. It is not that the world comes under control, but that our own actions and those of others with whom we construct mutual plans become, within limits, predictable and comprehensible, so that we may rely on ourselves and others.

Keith Oatley

General Sources for the Book (FOP) Overall

Ackroyd, P. (1990). *Dickens.* New York, NY: HarperCollins.

Bandura, A. (1990). Conclusion: Reflections on nonability determinants of competence. In R.J. Sternberg & J. Kolligan (Eds.), *Competence considered.* New Haven, CT: Yale University Press.

Barron, F. (1963). *Creativity and mental health.* Princeton, NJ: Van Nostrand.

Baumeister, R.F., & Scher, S.J. (1988). Self-defeating behavior patterns among normal individuals: Review and analysis of common self-destructive tendencies. *Psychological Bulletin, 104,* 3-22.

Baumeister, R.F., Heatherton, T.F., & Tice, D.M. (1994). *Losing control.* New York, NY: Academic Press.

Boice, R. (1992). Combined treatments for writing blocks. *Behaviour Research and Therapy, 30,* 107-116.

Boice, R. (1993a). Primal origins and later correctives for midcareer disillusionment. *New Directions for Teaching and Learning, 55,* 33-41.

Boice, R. (1993b). Writing blocks and tacit knowledge. *Journal of Higher Education, 64,* 19-54.

Boice, R. (1994). *How writers journey to comfort and fluency: A psychological adventure.* Westport, CT: Praeger.

Boice, R. (1995). Writerly rules for teachers. *Journal of Higher Education, 66,* 32-60.

Boice, R. (1996a). Classroom incivilities. *Research in Higher Education,* in press.

Boice, R. (1996b). *Procrastination and blocking.* Westport, CT: Praeger.

Bond, M.J, & Feather, N.T. (1988). Some coordinates of structure and purpose in the use of time. *Journal of Personality and Social Psychology, 55,* 321-329.

Bond, M.J, & Feather, N.T. (1988). Some coordinates of structure and purpose in the use of time. *Journal of Personality and Social Psychology, 55,* 321-329.

Bowers, P. (1979). Hypnosis and creativity: The search for the missing link. *Journal of Abnormal Psychology, 88,* 564-572.

Brand, A.G. (1986). *The psychology of writing: The affective experience.* Westport, CT: Greenwood.

Bruer, J.T. (1993). The mind's journey from novice to expert. *American Educator, 17*(2), 6-16 & 38-45.

Burka, J.B., & Yuen, L.M. (1983). *Procrastination.* Reading, MA: Addison-Wesley.

Charlton, J. (1986). *The writer's quotation book.* New York, NY: Viking Penguin.

Csikszentmihalyi, M. (1990). *Flow: The psychology of optimal experience.* New York, NY: Harper & Row.

Elbow, P. (1973). *Writing without teachers.* New York, NY: Oxford University Press.

Ellenberger, H. (1970). *The discovery of the unconscious .* New York, NY: Basic Books.

Ellis, A., & Knaus, W.J. (1977). *Overcoming procrastination.* New York, NY: Institute for Rational Living.

Ericsson, K.A., & Charness, N. (1994). Expert performance: Its structure and acquisition. *American Psychologist, 49,* 725-747.

Field, J. (1981) *A life of one's own.* Los Angeles, CA: J.P. Tarcher. (Originally published 1936.)

Flower, L. (1990). The role of task representation in reading-to-write. In L. Flower, V. Stein, J. Ackerman, M.J. Kantz, K. McCormick, & W.C. Peck. (Eds.), *Reading-to-write.* New York, NY: Oxford University Press.

Gardner, H. (1993). *Creating minds.* New York, NY: Basic Books.

Glendinning, V. (1992). *Anthony Trollope.* New York, NY: Knopf.

Hayes, J.R., & Flower, L.S. (1986). Writing research and the writer. *American Psychologist, 41,* 1106- 1113.

Jamison, K.R. (1993). *Touched with fire.* New York, NY: Free Press.

Jasen, D.A. (1981). *P.G. Wodehouse: A portrait of a master.* New York, NY: Continuum.

Kabat-Zinn, J. (1994). *Wherever you go, there you are.* New York, NY: Hyperion.

Kellogg, R.T. (1994). *The psychology of writing.* New York, NY: Oxford.

Langer, E.J. (1989). *Mindfulness.* Reading, MA: Addison-Wesley.

Meichenbaum, D. (1985). Teaching thinking: A cognitive-behavioral perspective. In S.F. Chipman & J.W. Segal (Eds.), *Thinking and Learning Skills,* vol. 2, 407-426. Hillsdale, NJ: Erlbaum.

Mills, C.W. (1959). *The sociological imagination.* New York, NY: Grove Press.

Moxley, J. (1992). *Publish, don't perish.* Westport, CT: Praeger.

Murray, D.M. (1978). Write before writing. *College Composition and Communication, 29,* 375-381.

Murray, D. (1995). *The craft of revision.* New York, NY: Harcourt Brace.

Nixon, H.K. (1928). *Psychology for the writer.* New York, NY: Harper.

Oatley, K. (1992). *Best laid schemes: The psychology of emotions.* New York, NY: Cambridge University.

Olsen, T. (1965). *Silences.* New York, NY: Delacorte.

Olson, G.A. (1992). Publishing scholarship in humanistic disciplines: Joining the conversation. In J. Moxley (Ed.), *Writing and publishing,* 49-69. New York, NY: University Press of America.

Perkins, D.N. (1981). *The mind's best work.* Cambridge, MA: Harvard University Press.

Perl, J. (1994). *Sleep right in five nights.* New York, NY: William Morrow.

Rabinbach, A. (1990). *The human motor.* New York, NY: Basic Books.

Rothblum, E.D. (1990). The fear of failure: The psychodynamic, need achievement, fear of success, and procrastination models. In H. Leitenberg (Ed.), *Handbook of social and evaluation anxiety,* 387-394. New York, NY: Plenum.

Seligman, M.E.P. (1991). *Learned optimism.* New York, NY: Knopf.

Skinner, B.F. (1981). How to discover what you have to say—a talk to students. *The Behavior Analyst, 4,* 1-7.

Simonton, D.K. (1994). *Greatness.* New York, NY: Guilford.

Singer, J.L. (1988). Sampling ongoing unconsciousness and emotional implications for health. In M.J. Horowitz (Ed.), *Psychodynamics and cognition,* 297-348. Chicago, IL: University of Chicago Press.

Smith, A. (1776). *The wealth of nations.* Oxford, England: Clarendon Press.

Snyder, C.R., & Higgins, R.L. (1988). Excuses: Their effective role in the negotiation of reality. *Psychological Bulletin,104,* 23-35.

Sternberg, R.J., Okagaki, L., & Jackson, A.S. (1990). Practical intelligence for success in school. *Educational Leadership,42,* 35-39.

Strunk, W., & White, E.B. (1979). *The elements of style.* New York, NY: Macmillan.

Tremmel, R. (1989). Investigating productivity and other factors in the writer's practice. *Freshman English News,17,* 19-25.

Tremmel, R. (1993). Zen and the art of reflective practice in teacher education. *Harvard Educational Review, 63,* 434-468.

Trollope, A. (1929). *An autobiography.* Boston, MA: Houghton Mifflin.

Wallace, I. (1968). *The writing of one novel.* New York, NY: Simon and Schuster.

Indices

INDEX OF PERSONS